What Your Colleagues Are

MW00335515

"*Schools on the Move* details how leaders can create clarity, develop collective expertise, and promote continuous improvement, all aimed at taking action to achieve equitable growth in student learning. You feel the momentum, you want to get on board, and the examples show how to get schools moving."

—**John Hattie**, Emeritus Laureate Professor at
Melbourne Graduate School of Education and Chair,
Board of the Australian Institute for Teaching and School Leadership

"*Schools on the Move* provides a clear and compelling portrait of what it takes to move schools toward continuous improvement. Westover and Steinhauser offer insights into how to overcome problems of practice that too often thwart improvement efforts. This will be an invaluable resource for how to bring about genuine and sustainable change."

—**Pedro A. Noguera**, Dean of USC Rossier School of Education

"*Schools on the Move* presents a framework for improvement and equity embedded in the ongoing work of educators. You will find tools designed to help develop the clarity of focus, shared leadership, collective expertise, and continuous improvement culture, but it is through the real-life examples of specific schools and districts that the framework comes alive."

—**Jennifer O'Day**, Institute Fellow at the
American Institutes for Research

"Jay Westover and Chris Steinhauser provide a clear and practical roadmap to address inequitable student learning and reimagine schools for the next decades. Filled with thoughtful analysis, case studies, and practical tips and tools this book is a powerful call to collaborative and precise action for all educators—a must-read reference to guide current and future work in our schools."

—**Mary Jean Gallagher**, Chief Student Achievement Officer and
Assistant Deputy Minister (retired),
Ministry of Education for Ontario, Canada

"With keen insights and clear prose, Jay Westover and Chris Steinhauser show leaders how to frame improvement initiatives as dynamic theories of action engaging staff members in collective reflection of their current practice, shared identification of opportunities to adopt and adapt better practices, and taking collective action to develop precision without prescription. *Schools on the Move* is a must-read guide for school and district leaders who understand that success is not a destination, but a journey."

—**Bryan Goodwin**, President & CEO at McREL International

"Jay Westover and Chris Steinhauser have done an excellent job in their design of a concrete framework for school improvement. These compelling examples will help readers in understanding that, despite challenging circumstances, they too can achieve equitable outcomes for students."

—**Jenni Donohoo**, bestselling author and education consultant

"Westover and Steinhauser provide leaders a road map for building the collective efficacy needed to transform learning outcomes for millions of students. Their findings are clear, actionable, and powerful."

—**Joseph F. Johnson, Jr.**, Executive Director, National Center for Urban School Transformation and Emeritus Dean and Professor, College of Education San Diego State University

"I was not surprised to see Jay Westover and Chris Steinhauser collaborating. Jay's 'On the Move' work has been utilized by superintendents across the country to focus on key drivers and to intentionally improve their districts. Steinhauser had historic tenure and influence at one of the largest school districts in the country in the battle against systemic inequities and the liberation of students. This is a necessary resource for site, district, and county educators."

—**Wesley Smith**, Superintendent of Newport-Mesa Unified School District and former Executive Director, Association of California School Administrators

"Equity and justice are long overdue in school systems. Westover and Steinhauser have provided a roadmap based on the idea of eliminating the variances between classrooms, schools, and districts so that every student, no matter where they are located, will get whatever they need to be successful."

—**David Cash**, Professor of Clinical Education and EDL Program Governance Chair at USC Rossier School of Education

"When Chris Steinhauser, one of the most successful and respected urban superintendents, joins forces with Jay Westover, a highly experienced and impactful education consultant, the result is a book worth reading by all education leaders. Our students deserve an education that reduces inequities and accelerates learning for all, and *Schools on the Move* is an invaluable resource for making this promise a reality."

—**Paul Gothold**, Superintendent of San Diego County Office of Education

"Steinhauser and Westover offer an approach for improvement based on factors that educators can control – climate, culture, capacity, and coherence. They put the educators in the driver's seat and give them a roadmap for continuous improvement that ensures all students receive high-quality educational opportunities."

—**Laura Schwalm**, former Superintendent of Garden Grove Unified School District

"Chris Steinhauser has long been considered a maven among his peers and a stalwart advocate for urban education. This insightful compilation of strategies is a must-read for school and district leaders. We must not miss this opportunity to reimagine public education."

—**Barbara Jenkins**, Superintendent of Orange County Public Schools

"This is the right book at the right time. Westover and Steinhauser brilliantly adapted *Schools on the Move* for this moment in time as we attempt to fight a global pandemic and the devastating impact it's having on our students, schools, and districts. I found dozens of ideas that I'll immediately be using because of this important work."

—**Rick Miller**, CEO of CORE Districts and former Deputy State Superintendent, California Department of Education

"Merging Westover's transformational work over the past 20 years helping school and district teams achieve equitable growth in student learning with Steinhauser's leadership and lessons learned in Long Beach USD, education leaders are provided clear and specific examples with tools, resources, and vignettes grounded in collective efficacy and continuous improvement."

—**Tom Armelino**, Executive Director (retired), California Collaborative for Educational Excellence

"We all need this book to understand the complexities of transforming climate, developing culture, building capacity, and creating coherence in our schools. Jay Westover and Chris Steinhauser show us how to recognize the potential in people and ideas and shape a common mindset. *Schools on the Move* is a pragmatic and reflective leadership guide using collaborative inquiry as a process to develop collective teacher efficacy. Being part of *Schools on the Move* has uniquely positioned our district during this time of rapid change to address and advance student learning."

—**Vivian Ekchian**, Superintendent of Glendale Unified School District

"*Schools on the Move* is a practical road map for school and district leaders to create cycles of collective inquiry, allowing for coherent improvement of student learning experiences. The storytelling is very effective, allowing us to see our own schools, districts, and leadership through this model."

—**Stefanie Phillips**, former Superintendent of Santa Ana Unified School District; CEO of Chamberlin Education Foundation

"A must-read for all those interested in transforming our systems to benefit all students and help them reach their fullest potential. Jay Westover and Chris Steinhauser use case studies to get to the heart of how to create coherent systems of continuous improvement focused on equitable growth in student learning. The attention to student learning variability and what to do with data shows us how these transformations are achievable."

—**Jorge Aguilar**, Superintendent of Sacramento City Unified School District

"Jay Westover and Chris Steinhauser identify and prioritize action steps to positively impact student outcomes. The combination of research studies, theory, practical applications, and success stories makes this book a must-read for all educational leaders!"

—**Don Austin**, Superintendent of Palo Alto Unified School District

"This timely book is filled with proven organizational principles, intentional practices, and frameworks for school leaders who are serious about building long-lasting sustainable success, and a culture of championship behaviors. Jay Westover and Chris Steinhauser share personal insights and examples from successful leaders, schools, and districts which continually seek clarity, collective inquiry, and build capacity to tackle the complex issues we face in our schools."

—**Sam Buenrostro**, Superintendent of Corona-Norco Unified School District

"School improvement is the most critical factor for student equity, access, and achievement. Jay Westover and Chris Steinhauser provide great examples of how this is successfully being done within various schools. This is a must-read for any educational leader who is serious about school improvement that leads to focused, continuous, and long-term growth in student learning."

—**Bill Crean**, Superintendent of Little Lake City School District

"Jay Westover and Chris Steinhauser outline how to leverage climate and culture to build shared leadership resulting in stronger collective teacher efficacy, increased student achievement, and greater equity. This isn't about a program or a silver bullet, it's about robust collaborative inquiry and dialogue system-wide that centers on evidence of impact for all students; it's about creating a true professional learning organization."

—**Dave Olney**, Superintendent of Hesperia Unified School District

"The thoughtfulness of this text is a refreshing approach. *Schools on the Move* reinforces the importance of taking time to see and analyze the problem and the associated systems prior to implementing a change idea. I have great appreciation for the strategy of inclusivity among those closest to the work."

—**Christi Barrett**, Superintendent of Hemet Unified School District

Schools on the Move

We dedicate this book to the education community for their resolve, resilience, and resourcefulness in navigating this next normal in education.

LIBRARY OF
CONGRESS
SURPLUS
DUPLICATE

Schools on the Move

Leading Coherence for Equitable Growth

Jay Westover
and
Christopher Steinhauser

FOR INFORMATION:

Corwin

A SAGE Company

2455 Teller Road

Thousand Oaks, California 91320

(800) 233-9936

www.corwin.com

SAGE Publications Ltd.

1 Oliver's Yard

55 City Road

London EC1Y 1SP

United Kingdom

SAGE Publications India Pvt. Ltd.

B 1/I 1 Mohan Cooperative Industrial Area

Mathura Road, New Delhi 110 044

India

SAGE Publications Asia-Pacific Pte. Ltd.

18 Cross Street #10-10/11/12

China Square Central

Singapore 048423

President: Mike Soules

Vice President and
    Editorial Director: Monica Eckman

Senior Acquisitions
    Editors: Ariel Curry and Tanya Ghans

Content Development
    Manager: Desirée A. Bartlett

Senior Editorial Assistant: Caroline Timmings

Editorial Assistants: Nancy Chung and
                      Nyle De Leon

Production Editor: Tori Mirsadjadi

Copy Editor: Pam Schroeder

Typesetter: C&M Digitals (P) Ltd.

Cover Designer: Candice Harman

Marketing Manager: Morgan Fox

Copyright © 2022 by Corwin Press, Inc.

All rights reserved. Except as permitted by U.S. copyright law, no part of this work may be reproduced or distributed in any form or by any means, or stored in a database or retrieval system, without permission in writing from the publisher.

When forms and sample documents appearing in this work are intended for reproduction, they will be marked as such. Reproduction of their use is authorized for educational use by educators, local school sites, and/or noncommercial or nonprofit entities that have purchased the book.

All third-party trademarks referenced or depicted herein are included solely for the purpose of illustration and are the property of their respective owners. Reference to these trademarks in no way indicates any relationship with, or endorsement by, the trademark owner.

Printed in Canada

Library of Congress Cataloging-in-Publication Data

Names: Westover, Jay Allen, author. | Steinhauser, Christopher, author.

Title: Schools on the move : leading coherence for equitable growth / Jay Westover and Christopher Steinhauser.

Description: Thousand Oaks, California : Corwin, 2022. | Includes bibliographical references and index.

Identifiers: LCCN 2021060074 | ISBN 9781071822449 (Paperback : acid-free paper) | ISBN 9781071822432 (ePub) | ISBN 9781071822418 (ePub) | ISBN 9781071822401 (PDF)

Subjects: LCSH: School improvement programs—United States. | Educational change—United States.

Classification: LCC LB2822.82 .W3777 2022 | DDC 371.2/07—dc23/eng/20220202
LC record available at https://lccn.loc.gov/2021060074

This book is printed on acid-free paper.

22 23 24 25 26 10 9 8 7 6 5 4 3 2 1

DISCLAIMER: This book may direct you to access third-party content via web links, QR codes, or other scannable technologies, which are provided for your reference by the author(s). Corwin makes no guarantee that such third-party content will be available for your use and encourages you to review the terms and conditions of such third-party content. Corwin takes no responsibility and assumes no liability for your use of any third-party content, nor does Corwin approve, sponsor, endorse, verify, or certify such third-party content.

Contents

Foreword

by Michael Fullan

Take one of the longest-serving successful superintendents since the turn of the century (Chris Steinhauser) and an engaged, effective external consultant to schools and districts (Jay Westover) during that same 20+ years. Then partner them and find out what they have learned and now recommend to schools for moving forward in the 2020s decade. What you get is clear, powerful analysis and advice set for action. Most of all the ideas are clear, comprehensive, and loaded with tips and tools for action in every chapter.

The concepts are well defined, deep, and nestled with other insights that simultaneously set up comprehensive understanding and immediate action. The foundation chapter consists of four Cs: climate (beliefs), capacity (efficacy), culture (behaviors), and coherence (shared depth of understanding). They start with root causes of variance—under what conditions schools succeed and fail—and readily identify why achievers (like Steinhauser and his team) succeed.

The authors use a small number of organizing schema that guide the reader through understanding and action, such as the key drivers: clarity of focus, shared leadership, continuous improvement, and collective expertise. In all cases they get into detail: what to do and how to do it. They use hypothetical districts that feel like real cases because they are based on districts that Westover and his team worked with or examples from Steinhauser's Long Beach Unified, which he led successfully for 18 years. We encounter a series of key issues and the sequence that results in solutions: who are the students who are struggling, what are the root cause of inequity, how can we collectively seek out and apply practices that improve learning, and how can we apply these proven practices to achieve growth for all students?

They then capture and take us through the steps and actions related to what they call "navigating a coherent path of school improvement." The steps have the appropriate degree of complexity as it becomes evident that the actions are not straightforward. For me the analysis and advice have just the right degree of understanding and doubt. The reader understands that there are many things to contend with but gets a good sense about what needs to be done because the core concepts provide particular support in terms of each concept itself and show appropriate connection to other key factors.

There are also a lot of feedback loops: How does evidence of impact guide design? How does evidence of impact link to refining achievement efforts? How do you refine recurring collaborative inquiry cycles? Great attention is paid to how to begin, doubling back to continually refine clarity of purpose, and using end points to clarify how to get increased inputs. I found it also valuable to have specific insights into how Long Beach sustained improvement efforts. We see the role of a powerful five-part graduate profile that encompassed five elements, including adaptive and productive citizenship, innovative problem-solving, and the like.

The book is full of posing difficult challenges and directional solutions, such as how you get coherence while avoiding prescription, how collaboration and coherence can go together, and how to zero in on assessing impact. Frameworks are provided as guidelines to action, and then they are applied to case examples of the factors in practice, including results obtained. In each chapter there are tips and tools for action that include: guiding principles, student learning priorities, short-term actionable plans, and collaborative inquiry cycles that show the action as it occurs through a sequence of analyze, design, implement, and refine—complete with success indicators, supports, evidence of learning, and timeframes.

Like my own work (exemplified in the case studies of the book *Nuance* (Corwin 2019)), Westover and Steinhauser show that complex success can be accomplished only through joint determination and related to shared leadership at the school and the district levels. Mobilizing ongoing, focused, cumulative, collaborative improvement is the essence of success. For these authors, collective impact is the test. In all of this work the authors attempt to be clear and specific as well as reflective. They center on collaborative culture, leadership capacity, and impact on school improvement—accompanied by questions to be considered. Then we see different examples of schools engaged in the path of progress as they play out in different contexts. After several case studies the authors review the lessons learned under the rubric of tips and tools for taking action including a planning template.

All and all *Schools on the Move* is devoted to developing cultures of collective expertise within schools and districts and their interactions. They discuss and portray successes and failures: what to do when groups are compliant, resistant, or fragmented and ultimately how to cultivate cultures of instructional coherence. Particularly valuable is the case study of Long Beach Unified School District (LBUSD) with its 84 schools that built a culture of sustained coherence with Steinhauser as superintendent over a period of 18 years. We see the internal dynamics of LBUSD as it went about building, fostering, and sustaining a robust culture of collaborative inquiry linked to continuing results. Carefully documented is what the authors call "visible evidence of student learning" along with details of the paths of progress in particular schools. We see clearly how LBUSD created instructional coherence across its schools with in-depth case accounts in several individual schools.

In sum this is a book whose authors, together, are clearly comfortable cycling back and forth between the macro and micro levels and their interconnections. In the best books on school systems, practice drives theory as much as the other way around. We are in the hands of two authors who have distilled their knowledge from the last 20 years of intense improvement work and have given the best of their insights. It is practical and theoretical and provides heaps of help for those on or about to journey into the unknown of school system change.

Preface

The writing of *Schools on the Move* began in the fall of 2019 to address the underlying factors that influence the impact of school improvement efforts. *Districts on the Move* had previously been written to assist school districts with leading systemic improvement by shaping culture, building capacity, and creating coherence. However, district improvement efforts do not always account for the variances in climate, culture, capacity, and coherence that exist within and among school sites. For this reason, *Schools on the Move* was to be a resource for school leaders to navigate a coherent path of improvement for achieving equitable growth in student learning. However, in March 2020 the education community was faced with the greatest challenge of our lifetime: the COVID-19 pandemic. Within a short period of time almost all schools in the United States were closed, and then most reemerged in a distance learning modality. The concept of moving school sites forward in support of equitable growth in student learning needed to be reframed in light of this massive disruption to the education system.

At this time, Jay refocused his efforts on the urgent topic of "navigating the next normal in education." An approach for school district and site leaders to guide improvement efforts during the pandemic was shaped as phases that emulated the guidance for business leaders provided by McKinsey: resolve, resilience, return, reimagination, and reculturing (Sneader & Singhal, 2020). Figure 0.1 depicts these five phases for educators to navigate a path of progress in this new normal. As the pandemic progressed, teachers adapted to supporting student learning through new modalities, and leaders adjusted improvement strategies to meet the demands of a different context for supporting teaching and learning. For many school districts and sites, the chaos and disruption brought on by the pandemic was seen as an opportunity to reimagine education for the betterment of all students and re-culture schools to embrace more innovative approaches for overcoming student equity issues and deepening student learning.

Figure 0.1   The Five Phases for Navigating the Next Normal in Education

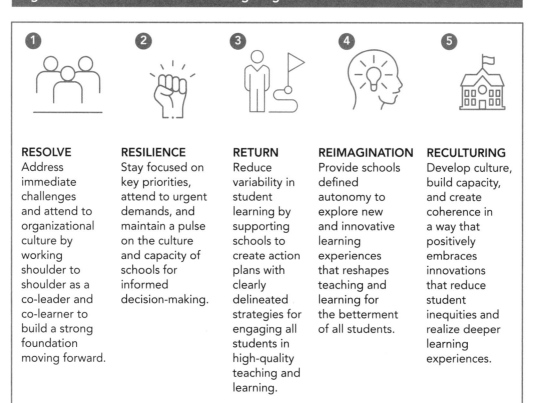

RESOLVE	**RESILIENCE**	**RETURN**	**REIMAGINATION**	**RECULTURING**
Address immediate challenges and attend to organizational culture by working shoulder to shoulder as a co-leader and co-learner to build a strong foundation moving forward.	Stay focused on key priorities, attend to urgent demands, and maintain a pulse on the culture and capacity of schools for informed decision-making.	Reduce variability in student learning by supporting schools to create action plans with clearly delineated strategies for engaging all students in high-quality teaching and learning.	Provide schools defined autonomy to explore new and innovative learning experiences that reshapes teaching and learning for the betterment of all students.	Develop culture, build capacity, and create coherence in a way that positively embraces innovations that reduce student inequities and realize deeper learning experiences.

© 2022 InnovateEd

Icon sources: Resolve from BestForLater91/iStock.com; Resilience from Penti-Stock/iStock.com; Return from fonikum/iStock.com; Reimagination from da-vooda/iStock.com; Reculturing from LysenkoAlexander/iStock.com

In February 2021, Jay and Chris met to discuss how the book could be written to best serve educators in light of the pandemic. The once-in-a-lifetime opportunity for reimagining and re-culturing education to overcome the prevailing, and now intensified, student equity issues became a moral imperative for the writing of this book. Chris had recently retired after serving as superintendent of LBUSD for 18 years. During his tenure the district had been recognized for sustainable and systemic improvement that achieved equitable growth in student learning within all school sites. His depth of knowledge and experience with leading systemic improvement to close student equity gaps is unparalleled among education leaders. And so the research and practices from the work that Jay had undertaken in partnership with school districts were merged with the long-term success and deep impact of the work Chris led in Long Beach to create a framework for schools to be on the move.

The concept of schools on the move should be considered as the way in which teachers and leaders transform climate, shape culture, build capacity, and create coherence to achieve equitable growth in student learning. Prior to the pandemic, the four key drivers of school improvement had been framed as clarity of focus, shared leadership, collective expertise, and continuous improvement. And now, almost 2 years after the pandemic unfolded, these four key drivers are of even greater importance for teachers and leaders to guide school improvement efforts. As education is reimagined for the betterment of all students and schools are re-cultured to embrace innovative approaches for accelerating student learning, our hope is that *Schools on the Move* serves as a valuable resource for navigating this next normal.

Acknowledgments

The inspiration for writing this book was two decades in the making as the years of supporting systemic district improvement have revealed that school districts cannot be "on the move" if school sites within them do not have the climate, culture, capacity, or coherence needed to sustain the equitable growth in student learning. Over this period of time I have had the pleasure of partnering with school districts that aspired to be a district on the move as well as individual schools whose staff desired to be part of a school on the move. The common theme that has emerged from this collaborative work is that to be on the move requires clarity of focus, shared leadership, collective expertise, and continuous improvement. It is rare to see these four key drivers in action within a school district or site, and so, I want to recognize and commend the education systems that have navigated the complexities of systemic improvement. These are Local District Northwest in Los Angeles Unified School District, Corona-Norco USD, Hesperia USD, Santa Monica-Malibu USD, Santa Barbara USD, Norwalk USD, Rialto USD, Palmdale USD, Moreno Valley USD, Ukiah USD, Desert Sands USD, Santa Rosa City Schools, Gateway Community Charter Schools, Arvin School District, Rosedale School District, Little Lake City School District, La Habra City Schools, and Kern County Office of Education. Because this work requires a village of deep expertise, much has been learned along the way by collaborating with the exceptional team at InnovateEd, Michael Fullan, Mary Jean Gallagher, Joanne Quinn, the Association of California School Administrators, the California Collaborative for Educational Excellence, and Kansas MTSS and Alignment. I would be remiss not to thank Ariel Curry for her astute ability as an editor to guide Chris and me in shaping the book to become a valuable resource for educators. Last, this book was put on hiatus as the COVID-19 pandemic unfolded, and its resurgence—and completion—was made possible when Chris Steinhauser agreed to be my co-author. Chris is recognized as one of the most successful, knowledgeable, and humble education leaders in the nation. His keen insights and practical experience brought this book to life so that the "Long Beach Way" can serve as a north star for navigating the next normal in education. His collaboration and friendship are greatly appreciated.

—Jay Westover

There are so many people to thank for supporting me on my educational journey and the opportunity to co-author this book with Jay Westover. First and foremost my parents for giving me the love of learning and instilling in me that anything is possible if I worked hard enough to achieve it. To my wife Alida, my son Edward and his wife Haley, my daughter Patricia and her husband Dan and their two children CJ and Ava, thank you for all the love, support, and encouragement you have given me over the years to be an equity champion for our most vulnerable students. To my LBUSD family, thank you for what you do each and every day to ensure that every youth in your care is given the tools they need to be college and career ready upon graduation. Your commitment to equity and closing achievement and opportunity gaps is beyond reproach. You have shown the nation and the world that urban school districts can be models of excellence when meeting the needs of our most vulnerable students and their families. To the Board of Education members that hired me in 2002 and supported me as their superintendent for 18 years, thank you for believing in me and demonstrating to the nation what effective board–superintendent governance looks like. A special thank you to Lori Grady, Juan Guiterrez, Tammy Lavelle, Connie Magee, and Alejandro Vega for sharing your stories of how you use the collaborative inquiry process to transform your schools into models of excellence in meeting the needs of the whole child. To all the equity leaders in our nation (especially my LBUSD colleagues), thank you for keeping the moral imperative and civil rights issue of this century alive and well in your school systems and schools. Last but not least, I cannot thank Jay Westover enough for pushing me out of my comfort zone to assist him in writing *Schools on the Move*. Jay, I have learned so much from you and am blessed to have you as a colleague and friend.

—Christopher Steinhauser

About the Authors

Jay Westover has provided leadership training and school improvement consulting in collaboration with the U.S. Department of Education, state departments of education, colleges, educational service centers, and school districts across North America. Over the past 20 years, his work has focused on developing the capacity of school systems to close student equity and learning and performance gaps. Creating coherent systems of continuous improvement has been a central aspect of statewide, regional, and local partnerships that have supported more than 250 school districts nationwide. Jay's role at InnovateEd is lead advisor for client partnerships, and he also serves as an executive leadership coach. His passion is working alongside leaders to simplify the complexities of shaping culture, developing capacity, and creating coherence for sustainable improvement.

Christopher Steinhauser served as superintendent of the LBUSD from 2002 to 2020, the fourth-largest school district in California serving approximately 70,000 students. With more than 39 years of experience in the diverse Long Beach school system, Chris has earned a national reputation for improving student achievement and closing achievement and opportunity gaps. To ensure that there were equitable outcomes for all students in the school system, Chris implemented a continuous improvement process known as The Collaborative Inquiry Process/Quarterly Visits, in which teams of educators from different schools would visit each other's sites to review student outcome data and observe teaching and learning. The purpose of this process was to make real-time changes based on formative assessment data to better meet the diverse academic and social-emotional needs of the students in the system. These site visits would occur three to four times per year. Under his leadership, Long Beach earned the national Broad Prize for Urban Education and qualified as a finalist for the award five times. A 2010 report by McKinsey & Company named Long Beach as one of the world's 20 leading school systems—and one of the top 3 in the United States in terms of sustained and significant improvements. The school district was later listed among the world's top five school systems by the nonprofit Battelle for Kids organization.

Long Beach students, 70% of whom receive free and reduced-price lunches, annually earn more than $100 million in college scholarships. Thirteen Long Beach high schools were named in 2020 to be among the top 12% in the United States by *U.S. News and World Report*. Under Chris's leadership, the Long Beach College Promise was developed, which became a model for the State of California and the nation on providing 2 years of free college to every student who enrolled in a community college upon graduating from high school. Since the implementation of the Long Beach College Promise, the college-going rate for students in LBUSD has been consistently higher than the State of California and the nation. To ensure that all students were college and career ready upon graduation from high school, Chris implemented industry-based pathways system-wide through the Linked Learning approach to ensure equitable outcomes for all high school students.

Introduction

The book *Districts on the Move* (Westover, 2019) was jointly published by Corwin and InnovateEd to more clearly define the critical success factors and key leadership competencies for navigating systemic district improvement. Ultimately, the desired impact of this framework was to guide the sustainable improvement of leadership, teaching, and student learning. Four benchmarks served as guideposts for district and school leaders: creating clarity of district goals and school priorities for student learning, cultivating a culture of shared leadership and systemic collaboration, developing collective expertise with a coherent instructional framework, and engaging in evidence-based cycles of inquiry for continuous improvement.

It has been powerful to witness systemic improvement unfold through the collective efforts of district leaders, principals, and teachers. Transformations at the district and school levels central to this change process are shifting from fragmentation and overload to clarity of purpose, from discord to solidarity, and from compliance to connected autonomy. Irrespective of the differences in climate, culture, capacity, and coherence that exist among school districts, the catalyst for systemic improvement stems from shaping a common vision with shared depth of understanding for the work at hand: equitable growth in learning for all students.

This practitioner-oriented action research further brought to light the complexities of systemic improvement and revealed the most significant challenges facing school districts. The greatest influence on school district improvement is the extent to which school leaders and teachers collectively transform climate, develop culture, and build capacity for the purpose of creating coherence. At the heart of this matter is a foundational principle that schools are the unit of change for systemic improvement. It is imperative to reduce the variances in climate, culture, capacity, and coherence that exist among and within school sites if school districts are to create a coherent system of continuous improvement. This realization was the primary reason for writing this next book of the *–on the Move–* series: *Schools on the Move*.

If the inherent complexities of school climate, culture, capacity, and coherence are the building blocks for systemic district improvement, then the solution moving forward must be to simplify and focus improvement strategies. The research points to a promising practice with the greatest potential for schools, and that practice is developing collective efficacy through collaborative inquiry. When school climate and culture are driven by a collective commitment to develop collective expertise through robust collaborative inquiry processes, the result is steadfast growth in shared depth of understanding and precision of practice that accelerates learning for all students. At face value, this may not seem like a significant shift for schools and districts; however, the implications for leadership, teaching, and student learning are astounding when compared to the widely accepted practices that currently drive systemic improvement.

Even though it is a road less traveled, a path of progress for schools can be forged from the critical success factors and key leadership competencies found within the *Districts on the Move* framework. To this end, a simplified and focused improvement process has been defined by the four key drivers of school improvement: clarity of focus, shared leadership, collective expertise, and continuous improvement. In a nutshell, schools on the move demonstrate shared leadership focused on equitable growth in student learning that is driven by the continuous improvement of practices to develop collective expertise.

Problems of Practice (What We See)

For the past 15 years, Jay and the InnovateEd team have partnered with school districts to assist with developing capacity for the sustainable improvement of leadership, teaching, and student learning. Clear trends and patterns have emerged in working with district leaders, principals, and teachers to collectively create a coherent system of continuous improvement. These emergent problems of practice are central to the root causes of variance in student learning growth. Chris, in serving as superintendent of Long Beach Unified School District for an unheard-of 18 years, also witnessed similar trends and patterns in leading the work of 84 school sites. Throughout his tenure, the central office, in collaboration with school sites, created system-wide coherence and sustained improvement efforts through a laser-sharp focus on student equity.

> The greatest influence on school district improvement is the extent to which school leaders and teachers collectively transform climate, develop culture, and build capacity for the purpose of creating coherence.

Our collective findings may seem paradoxical because student inequity and underperformance are most often viewed from the vantage of inputs and outputs, meaning that we equate variance in student learning growth as being dependent on what John Hattie (2015) has phrased as "achieving at least one year of academic growth for every year of school." This is the two-sided coin of student demographics and academic performance often referenced as a pretext for growth in student learning, meaning that lower student socioeconomic status, language acquisition, and learning ability are equated with reduced academic performance: the parity of inequity and underperformance.

Schools on the move demonstrate shared leadership focused on equitable growth in student learning that is driven by the continuous improvement of practices to develop collective expertise.

We have found that the problems of practice associated with inequitable growth in student learning are not defined by inputs and outputs but rather emanate from school climate, culture, capacity, and coherence. It is important to make these root causes of variability more visible, and the best way to do so is through real-world examples and visuals that bring forth personal meaning. Climate is an outgrowth of beliefs and attitudes toward the work at hand. Culture is dependent upon the behaviors and actions in relation to the work at hand. Capacity is directly connected to confidence in the ability to do the work at hand. And coherence is relative to the shared depth and understanding of the work at hand. When put into context, the issues at hand become clear. As an example, if literacy were to be framed as a priority for achieving equitable growth in student learning, then we would assume that every school site within a school district would be equally compelled to focus on this student learning priority. However, the reality would be defined by the following:

1. Our beliefs and attitudes in regard to the moral imperative of student literacy

2. Our behaviors and actions in relation to supporting student literacy

3. Our confidence in the ability to improve student literacy

4. Our shared depth and understanding of high-yield student literacy strategies

We have witnessed these variances unfold through direct observation of the collaborative work among district leaders, principals, and teachers. And the research from Hattie (2015) in respect to between-school

(0.36) and within-school (0.64) variance in student learning growth is a mirror image of the inherent dynamics that occur during the improvement process. Every school district is unique in respect to climate, culture, capacity, and coherence, which in turn, has a significant influence on school sites. This is primarily a result of the interactions that occur within and among the district, school, and classroom levels. Linda Lambert (2003) has noted that "excellent schools in poor districts implode over time, whereas, poor schools in excellent districts get better over time." The same influences occur within each school site, but on a much larger scale due to the more frequent and personal interactions among principals, teachers, and students, it's more of a family affair—not to mention the impact of principals' leadership styles, experiences and expertise among teachers, variant student demographics, and the degree of family engagement. Dylan Wiliam (2018) may have phrased this issue best, "Today in America the biggest problem with education is not that it is bad. It is that it is variable. In hundreds of thousands of classrooms in America, students are getting an education that is as good as any in the world. But in hundreds of thousands of others, they are not."

If a school district were to define student literacy as the strategic focus for achieving equitable growth in student learning, then the influence of these four Cs needs to be taken into consideration for guiding systemic improvement. A climate expressed as "We already do literacy" and a culture that promotes "Tell us what to do, and we'll do it" will not result in forward movement of the student learning priority. And if capacity is defined by "I don't know how to support student literacy, and I don't want to learn how," and the current state of coherence is characterized as divergent and entrenched ideas of what constitutes student literacy, then there will be great difficulty navigating improvement efforts.

Figure i.1 illustrates the four root causes of variance: climate, culture, capacity, and coherence on district and school improvement. The attitudes, actions, capacity, and depth of understanding in relation to the work at hand will greatly influence the progress and improvement of student learning within a school or district. If any of these four root causes of variance are at odds with accelerating the learning of all students, then the rate of growth will be hampered or reduced. As a collective, these conditions can promote acceleration, stagnation, or regression of student learning results.

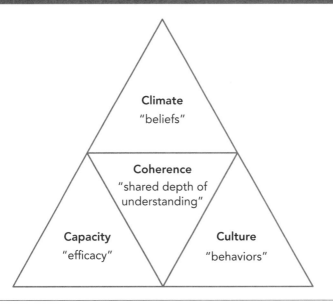

Figure i.1 Root Causes of Variance in Student Learning Growth

Climate
"beliefs"

Coherence
"shared depth of understanding"

Capacity
"efficacy"

Culture
"behaviors"

© 2022 InnovateEd

It is not sufficient to view these root causes at face value. Schools and districts must assess current reality in relation to the desired focus of improvement efforts if equitable growth in student learning is to be achieved. By simply framing the focus of improvement efforts within the context of the four Cs, the root causes of variance in student learning growth can be more clearly understood. This is the purpose of Figure i.2, reflecting on how improvement efforts are perceived among teachers and leaders. Climate and culture are tightly coupled in that beliefs affect behaviors. If I believe something is important or valuable, then my actions and behaviors will be positive and productive. If I don't see value or importance, then the result will be a resistant stance or a compliance orientation toward the work at hand. Similarly, capacity and coherence are interconnected by the simple fact that learning by doing to develop more expertise is the path that creates deeper understanding of the work at hand. And when the work is done collaboratively, a shared depth of understanding emerges. By pairing climate with culture and capacity with coherence, this simple tool provides a reality check of the current state of a school or district in relation to the work at hand. For example, if student literacy was the strategic focus for achieving equitable growth in student learning, then this resource can provide a sharp contrast of the root causes of variability in student learning that influence improvement efforts.

Figure i.2 Impact of the Root Causes of Variability on Student Learning Growth

Climate and Culture	Believers	Achievers
High	**Believers** Clarity of purpose Critical for all students Limited expertise Divergent schemas	**Achievers** Clarity of purpose Critical for all students Precision of practice Joint determination
	Doubters Competing priorities Essential for some students Limited expertise Fragmented and disjointed	**Idlers** Competing priorities Essential for some students Precision of practice Common schemas
Low	**Capacity and Coherence**	**High**

© 2022 InnovateEd

The four quadrants of doubters, believers, idlers, and achievers can be applied to the improvement efforts of a school district, individual school sites, or even groups or teams within a school. Doubters essentially are stuck in the status quo and struggle with competing priorities, lack of engagement, and false starts. Believers have a vision for improvement yet lack capacity and depth of understanding to move forward. Idlers have internal capacity and expertise but stagnate due to the lack of a collective commitment for the improvement of practices. And achievers are driven by a compelling vision and a desire to develop deep levels of collective expertise. Examples in context will be described in forthcoming chapters because these descriptions can apply to schools, leaders, and teachers alike. An interesting exercise is to consider recent or past improvement initiatives and use this tool to dissect the root causes of variability in the success, failure, or duration of these efforts. And the critical question is: "How do we best navigate these complex attributes that positively or negatively affect the continuous improvement of leadership, teaching, and student learning?"

The Research (What We Know)

If the goal is to ensure that for every year of school each student achieves at least a year of growth in learning, and that this desired outcome is influenced by between-school and within-school variance, then high-impact improvement strategies must focus on overcoming the sources of variance: climate, culture, capacity, and coherence. By design, the strategy must engage teachers with principals in the collective improvement of practices to accelerate learning for all students. Furthermore, district leaders need to be active participants so that school site support systems can be adapted and improved from this school-level work. Based on these criteria, the research points to collective teacher efficacy that has the highest effect size (1.39) on improving student learning outcomes (Hattie, 2018):

> Accomplishing the maximum impact on student learning depends on teams of teachers working together, with excellent leaders or coaches, agreeing on worthwhile outcomes, setting high expectations, knowing the students' starting and desired success in learning, seeking evidence continually about their impact on all students, modifying their teaching in light of this evaluation, and joining in the success of truly making a difference with student learning outcomes.

When this improvement strategy is closely examined to discern the fundamental components giving rise to such high levels of student learning growth, four key drivers are found to be at the core: clarity of focus, shared leadership, collective expertise, and continuous improvement. And the unifying factor that conjoins these four key drivers is collaborative inquiry (Figure i.3). This model can serve as a framework for educators who desire to develop collective teacher efficacy.

Figure i.3   Key Drivers for Achieving Equitable Growth in Student Learning

© 2022 InnovateEd

But how is collaborative inquiry associated with both reducing the root causes of student learning variance and guiding improvement efforts to achieve equitable growth in student learning? Collaborative inquiry provides the structure for educators to lead and learn together productively and, in so doing, develops distributed leadership, grows professional capital, increases collective efficacy, and focuses efforts on the causes of student success and failure (Donohoo & Velasco, 2016). The power of collaborative inquiry is that it *"shapes a common mindset,"* promoting improvement of practices and growth in student learning and, at the same time, providing a *"structured process for co-leading improvement efforts"* to achieve continual growth in learning for all students. The combined synergistic effect is that collaborative inquiry creates a common mindset with a structured process for co-leading improvement efforts.

Collaborative inquiry serves as both the catalyst that initiates forward motion and the fuel that sustains momentum.

In this manner, collaborative inquiry serves as both the catalyst that initiates forward motion and the fuel that sustains momentum. As is the case for any system, the activator of growth and continuous improvement must be introduced to the system for any action to occur. In other words, developing collective teacher efficacy is not an outcome but rather an inquiry process that must be initiated and sustained to have an impact on the growth and continuous improvement of student learning. We have found that the four key drivers (clarity of focus, shared leadership, collective expertise, and continuous improvement) serve as entry points for engaging in the process of collaborative inquiry to develop collective teacher efficacy. And once initiated, these four drivers feed off of each other to sustain collaborative inquiry cycles in pursuit of achieving equitable growth in student learning.

Clarity of focus may be the most critical driver when considering that research points to the fact that only 15% of staff can name the top three organizational goals (McChesney et al., 2016). The result is fragmentation, overload, and distractions that diminish the impact of improvement efforts on achieving growth in student learning (Fullan & Quinn, 2016a). Shared leadership plays a crucial role in the co-leading of improvement efforts. It is the collective efforts of teachers and principals with district leaders that shape the causal pathway linking learning priorities with student success indicators, high-yield pedagogical practices, and evidence of impact to achieve growth in learning for all students. Collective expertise is vital in that student learning is supported by the efforts of every teacher within a school, and if there is not precision of practices among all staff, the result is variance in student learning growth and improvement. And similarly, every student has different learning needs, and this requires the continuous adjustment and refinement of practices at the school and classroom levels to accelerate learning for all students.

So the compelling question is "Where to begin?" And the answer is that it depends on the climate, culture, capacity, and coherence of the school or district. To be more specific in defining potential action steps, the concept of believers, achievers, doubters, and idlers needs to be revisited. First, it is safe to assume that achievers would take action immediately to engage in collaborative inquiry and advance the four key drivers of improvement. It is for this reason that continuous improvement is the best entry point due to the comfort and familiarity with changing practices to improve results by getting better every day. The positive climate and productive culture of believers would certainly promote taking action at a slower pace by emphasizing shared leadership. And the collective expertise among the idlers could be leveraged to overcome the uncertainty as to whether collaborative efforts can positively affect learning outcomes for all students. Doubters have the steepest hill to climb because inaction over time has created great resistance to change and a culture of isolated practices that advocates for defending the status quo. However, the driver with the highest potential for doubters is creating clarity of focus because this leads to "working smarter, not harder." It should be noted that this is not a prescriptive recipe for success but rather what has been noted by Fritz (2011) as the path of least resistance that provides the best route for forward motion among a set of alternative options. Ultimately, all four drivers of improvement need to be actualized through a collaborative inquiry stance.

It is timely that a transformation in education is shifting from a reliance on *translating research into practice* toward *practitioner action research* that more clearly defines a path of progress and promotes the sharing of promising practices. A quote from Fullan (2016) that resonates with this shift is the phrase "find your own Finland." The implied meaning is that creating a coherent system of continuous improvement is influenced by the root causes of student learning variability (climate, culture, capacity, and coherence), guided by a systemic improvement process (clarity of focus, shared leadership, collective expertise, and continuous improvement), and driven by a common appreciation for the power of collaborative inquiry.

Promising Practices
(What to Do and How to Do It)

According to Bandura (1997), from whom the concept of collective efficacy originated, the best method to understand *what to do* and *how to do it* is to study those demonstrating success by way of vicarious learning experiences. Storytelling is the most powerful tool for gaining an understanding of complex topics and reconsidering closely held beliefs (Gallo, 2016). Stories in the form of case studies are the best instrument for applying these new ideas and concepts to real situations. So to bring promising practices to life, stories and case studies have been combined to inform actions at the classroom, school, and district levels.

To convey how school districts navigate the complexities of creating a coherent system of continuous improvement, the path of progress needs to be depicted from the perspectives of teachers, principals, and district leaders. To structure such a story, the collective efforts of school districts working with InnovateEd have been combined with the long-term success of Long Beach to illustrate the challenges, successes, barriers, and breakthroughs that are experienced at both the district office and among school sites. The journey of Anywhere School District and the endeavors of Somewhere School are integrated into the following chapters of the book as stories to create vicarious learning experiences. The primary purpose is to bring to light the root causes of between-school and within-school variance in student learning and enlighten the key drivers of improvement for accelerating growth in learning for all students.

Because the school site is the unit of change for systemic district improvement, the collective efforts of principals and teachers in the form of case studies provide in-depth and real-life scenarios for understanding the complexities of transforming climate, developing culture, building capacity, and creating coherence and also creates a viewpoint from which to gain essential insights for cultivating shared leadership, creating clarity of focus, developing collective expertise and guiding continuous improvement. Schools that have demonstrated ongoing progress with improvement of practices and sustained growth in student learning results have been selected as case studies embedded within the following chapters. Each case study includes a guide for in-depth analysis of problems of practice and promising practices to inform application by teachers, principals, and district leaders.

It has been noted that collaborative inquiry is both a mindset and a process for co-leading improvement efforts, and actionable tools provide the structured guidance needed to maneuver these nuanced endeavors. A collaborative inquiry cycle unfolds through the recurring sequence of analyze, design, implement, and refine (Westover, 2019). Analyze root causes of the problem to create a strategic focus for improvement efforts. Design high-impact strategies for building capacity to improve practices. Implement action steps with support, and adjust along the way. Refine improvement strategies based on evidence of impact. Collaborative inquiry tools that assist with the agile process of cultivating shared leadership, creating clarity of focus, developing collective expertise, and guiding continuous improvement have been included within each chapter to inform the work at the school site and district levels. These tools are paired with tips for action planning, leading implementation, and evaluating progress to sustain the improvement of practices and growth in learning for all students. In the following chapter we will lay the foundation as to how schools on the move navigate a coherent path of progress for achieving equitable growth in student learning.

The Pursuit of Equitable Growth in Student Learning

1

The diverse perspectives that exist among school staff, site leaders, district personnel, and community members create a compelling challenge when shaping a long-term vision of success. The simple question "What is our common vision for student success?" opens the flood gates and releases a deluge of opinions, beliefs, assumptions, and perceptions, which in turn can lead to a multitude of goals and initiatives with vague understanding and lack of commitment for the work at hand: achieving equitable growth in learning for all students. Under these circumstances, the famous phrase of Steve Jobs, "simplify and focus," rings true (Isaacson, 2011). An example of simplicity of focus in action was observed in working with Vivian Ekchian, superintendent of Glendale USD and former interim superintendent of Los Angeles USD, as evidenced by her compelling statement, "The work at hand is to identify the most struggling students in our schools, collectively determine how best to accelerate their learning, and apply these proven practices to achieve growth in learning for all students." Let's break this phrase down further into the most critical questions:

1. Who are the students in our schools who struggle most with learning?

2. What are the root causes of this inequity and underperformance among students?

3. How do we collectively seek out and learn from practices that improve student learning?

4. How can we apply these proven practices to achieve growth in learning for all students?

What if these four questions guided a commonly agreed-upon process that clarified student learning priorities and defined the collaborative work among all schools in a district? This certainly would shift the focus away from overarching goals and initiatives toward a focus driven by the continuous improvement of teaching and learning. Because the needs of students are unique to every school, such a process would provide defined autonomy coupled with accountability for student learning. Ultimately the outcome would be that every school site has created a clear and coherent path to attain growth in learning for all students. However, the quandary would be whether the leaders and teachers within each school have the shared depth of understanding and precision of practices to navigate such a path of progress. The purpose of the Schools on the Move framework is to resolve this complex issue faced by school districts and school sites: navigating a coherent path of progress.

Navigating a Coherent Path of Progress

School improvement is dependent upon how site leaders and teachers collectively create clarity of focus, cultivate shared leadership, develop collective expertise, and guide continuous improvement. And the linchpin is engaging in collaborative inquiry to establish a common mindset and structured process for co-leading these improvement efforts. The challenge is the natural tendency to focus on changing structures to improve the work at hand (i.e., roles, responsibilities, policies and procedures) rather than leading improvement processes that develop capacity to do the work at hand. This is akin to asking a novice driver to switch from an ordinary sedan to a race car and expecting that driving skills will improve by virtue of being in a superior automobile. A better approach is having a co-pilot in the passenger seat of the sedan with a clear focus on developing the expertise of the driver with feedback aimed at improving practices to yield better results and then transferring these much-improved practices to successfully drive the race car. Changing the structure without building capacity will not result in better performance.

It cannot be taken lightly how often the failure of school improvement efforts are due to the absence of a well-designed capacity-building strategy. The examples are boundless. A school staff becomes energized by the thought of becoming a professional learning community (PLC). And as a result, weekly collaboration time is allocated, essential standards are created, formative assessments are designed, low-performing students are identified, and tiered interventions are formalized. Then over time there is the realization that pedagogical practices have not changed, collaboration time is not used effectively, student learning supports are not being targeted or adjusted, and gains in student performance are not being realized. And soon PLCs no longer have the initial buzz and fade away to become a Wednesday event without clear purpose or impact. Sound familiar? The same scenario can apply to the adoption of new curriculum, training on research-based instructional strategies, a shift to project-based or personalized learning, a movement promoting social-emotional learning, and onward.

Schools that sustain improvement of practices and growth in student learning have harnessed the power of collaborative inquiry to navigate a path of progress using the four key drivers of school improvement; clarity of focus, shared leadership, collective expertise, and continuous improvement. These successful schools focus on learning "how to improve" rather than deciding "what to improve." The first step in navigating the journey of school improvement should be developing a common mindset among site leaders and teachers for co-leading the improvement of practices to realize equitable growth in student learning.

Figure 1.1 depicts collaborative inquiry as the connective tissue that binds together the four key drivers of school improvement. Critical success factors extend from each driver, which when attended to collectively, serve as a road map for site leaders and teachers to sustain improvement efforts. This is not a prescribed approach for checking off the boxes to arrive at a final destination. Rather, it is an ongoing and agile improvement process wherein site leaders and teachers continuously analyze, design, implement, and refine the work at hand.

The intent of this conceptual framework is to develop a common mindset and structured process for co-leading improvement efforts. And when actualized through the collective efforts of site leaders and teachers with support from district personnel, this becomes the foundation for schools to be on the move. For this forward movement to be realized, it is essential to begin with the end in mind. Mary Jean Gallagher, in gleaning from her years of experience with guiding systemic improvement around the world, has a simple phrase that gets to the heart of the matter; "In order for schools to improve, it is essential to develop a common understanding of what good looks like."

> Schools that sustain improvement of practices and growth in student learning have harnessed the power of collaborative inquiry to navigate a path of progress.

Figure 1.1　Navigating a Coherent Path of School Improvement

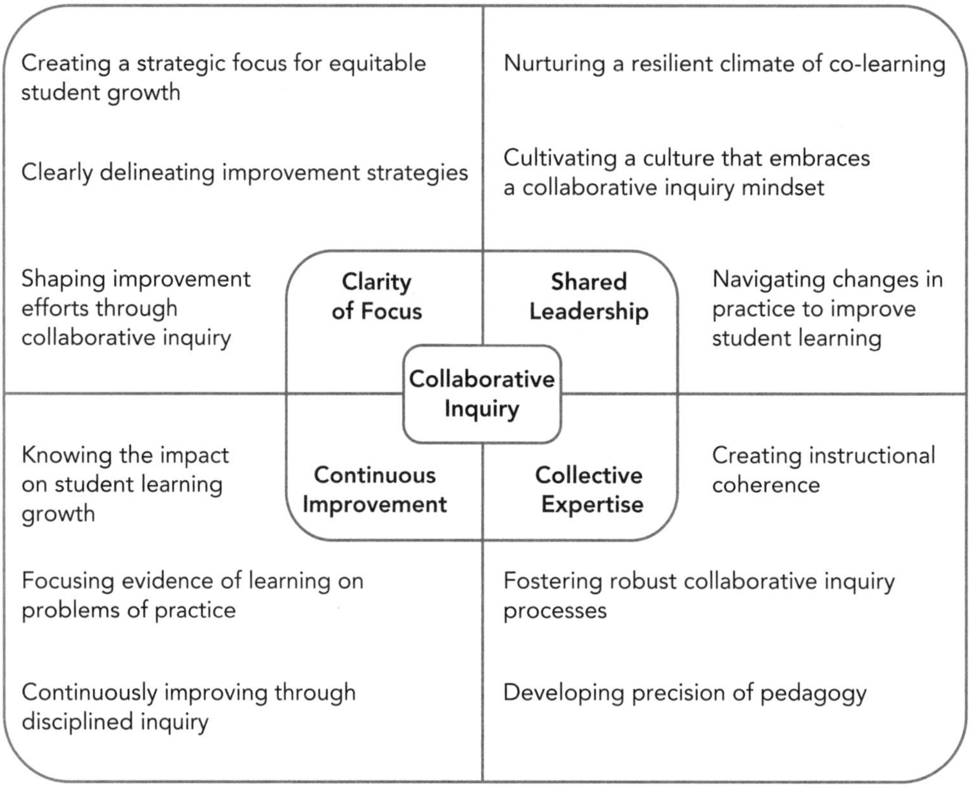

Creating a strategic focus for equitable student growth

Clearly delineating improvement strategies

Shaping improvement efforts through collaborative inquiry

Clarity of Focus

Shared Leadership

Collaborative Inquiry

Navigating changes in practice to improve student learning

Nurturing a resilient climate of co-learning

Cultivating a culture that embraces a collaborative inquiry mindset

Knowing the impact on student learning growth

Continuous Improvement

Collective Expertise

Creating instructional coherence

Focusing evidence of learning on problems of practice

Continuously improving through disciplined inquiry

Fostering robust collaborative inquiry processes

Developing precision of pedagogy

© 2022 InnovateEd

This is so true because most often there is a desire and pressure for improvement without a clear vision of success or the clarity needed to effectively navigate a coherent path of progress. Let's then shed light on what the key drivers and critical success factors for school improvement look like in action—in other words, "what good looks like."

Clarity of Focus

Creating clarity of focus has different meanings when considered from the context of teachers, site leaders, and district personnel. In finding common ground among all levels, the key is to ensure that the school focus is grounded in the daily work of students as they engage in learning at the classroom desk. Yet in reality, the sole purpose of having clarity of focus is to ensure that improvement efforts will overcome the root causes of variance in student learning occurring within and among classrooms. Another way of framing a strategic focus is in the form of a *theory of action*, or "if–then" statement, that by design is intended to overcome the *problems of practice* that are barriers to achieving growth in learning for all students. An example of a theory of action in practice would be focusing classroom instruction on student learning tasks that require close and analytic reading and evidence-based arguments so that all students develop improved literacy skills as part of daily instruction. In this fashion, if the school focus clearly defines the most critical factors for improving student learning at the classroom desk, then the result should be equitable growth in student learning.

However, this is a general statement for solving a complex problem and is the reason why clearly delineated improvement strategies are essential to create the *causal pathway* linking student success indicators with high-yield instructional practices informed by evidence. We would call this putting the theory of action into practice while seeking evidence of impact on student learning growth. This defines the most critical work at hand for developing shared depth and understanding of action steps moving forward. It is important to note that clarity of focus is achieved over time as precision of practices evolves to have greater impact on improving student learning. This requires that teachers and site leaders engage in recurring cycles of "learning by doing" shaped by a *collaborative inquiry* mindset and structured process extending over 6- to 9-week timeframes.

> A **strategic focus** for achieving equitable student growth guides school-wide improvement efforts with **clearly delineated improvement strategies** that take shape through the **ongoing collaborative work** among teachers and site leaders.

A few critical questions for consideration to create clarity of focus will be addressed in forthcoming chapters.

1. How can a theory of action guide school-wide improvement efforts to achieve equitable growth in student learning? (If we focus on this, then the result will be that.)

2. What problems of practice within and among classrooms could be the root cause of variance in student learning growth?

3. How can student success indicators be explicitly linked to high-yield instructional practices that are informed by evidence of impact on student learning?

4. How do a collaborative inquiry mindset and structured process for co-leading improvement efforts shape the ongoing work among teachers and site leaders?

Shared Leadership

Cultivating shared leadership may be one of the most misunderstood concepts in education and, therefore, is often underdeveloped and poorly attended to at both the district and school levels. This is primarily due to the fact that leadership is tightly coupled with navigating the inherent complexities of changing and improving climate (beliefs and attitudes) and culture (behaviors and actions). To cultivate shared leadership there must be common experiences that develop a shared belief and value for co-learning as the means of getting better together. And at the same time, collaboration structures and processes must be collectively shaped over time to establish common agreements for engaging in productive group work. Or to paraphrase Michael Fullan (2018), "Growing the capacity of the group to co-lead the improvement efforts of the group." Such an endeavor calls upon leaders to serve as lead learners that model co-learning, shape culture, and navigate changes in practices to improve student learning.

Clarifying what shared leadership looks like in action is best understood through examples and non-examples. The most often taken and least effective action is to focus on structural changes with predefined roles and responsibilities, which translates into overtaxing formal and informal leaders in the school to take on more work. This sounds like, "You're a good leader, so take on more leadership responsibilities," and conversely, "If you don't want to lead, then be a team player and do as you're told." This is not shared leadership but rather a hierarchical leadership structure. A more effective approach is to frame shared leadership in the form of a question, such as, "I wonder if we can work smarter and not harder by identifying our common challenges and dedicating time to work together on seeking solutions. I certainly don't have the answers but would greatly appreciate working together to see what we can collectively accomplish." Words like this, if spoken often enough and acted upon by formal and informal leaders, will begin to *nurture a climate of co-learning*.

> To cultivate shared leadership there must be common experiences that develop a shared belief and value for co-learning as the means of getting better together.

Culture is a harder nut to crack in that changing behaviors is the most challenging endeavor of any change process. Going back to ineffective actions, an often-seen strategy is to create structures for collaboration that include calendaring of dates with defined agendas, prescribed activities, and expectations to complete specific outcomes. The intent is that a structured process will promote effective collaboration, and that simply by participating, behaviors will change and ultimately result in productive group work. This only creates a compliance mentality, which further breeds frustration and resentment within and among groups. The unfortunate truth is that culture is cultivated and shaped as groups *embrace a collaborative inquiry mindset* for attending to the work at hand. Once again, a key question can be the catalyst for cultural change; "I wonder how we can come to know and understand which practices will yield the greatest impact on improving student learning in our school and classrooms?" In other words, culture is a mindset developed by collectively improving the work at hand and not a structured process that defines the actions and outcomes for doing the work at hand.

Changing practices should be easy now that climate is being nurtured and culture is being cultivated—right? Not so fast. There is a cartoon that beautifully illustrates the challenge of navigating changes in practice. A person stands at a podium in front of a crowd asking, "Who wants change?" And all raise their hands. Then they ask, "Who wants to change?" And all heads look down. And finally they ask, "Who wants to lead the change?" And the whole crowd quickly disperses. Therein lies the dilemma in that change is embraced until it affects us personally or necessitates us to lead the change process. The undertow preventing change from moving forward is fear of failure. So common sense would be to reduce anxiety and make success easily attainable, but that's not common practice. Unfortunately, the more common approach is a moral imperative for improvement with little clarity as to what to do better or how to do it effectively. For example, a principal might say, "Our number one priority is for all students to demonstrate growth in literacy and math proficiency." *Navigating changes in practice* requires a more nuanced approach wherein a few first followers initiate simple changes to realize short-term successes that quickly spread to others who want to experience the same success. And because success begets success, confidence, and willingness to overcome more complex changes follow suit. This is akin to starting an avalanche by rolling a snowball down a hill; start small and slow to go fast with increasing momentum.

> *Shared leadership is developed by nurturing a **climate of co-learning** and cultivating a **culture of collaborative inquiry**, which over time, builds the collective capacity needed to successfully **navigate changes in practice** for improving student learning results.*

A few critical questions for consideration to cultivate shared leadership will be addressed in forthcoming chapters.

1. How can the concept of "learning together to get better together" be modeled and promoted as part of daily work to nurture a resilient climate of co-learning?

2. How can the concept of "collaboratively seeking solutions to overcome the most common challenges at hand" be promoted to develop a collaborative inquiry mindset?

3. How can leadership structures, roles, and responsibilities be focused on developing collective capacity to navigate changes in practice within and among groups?

4. How can the pace of change and improvement of practices be attended to in a way that promotes "starting small and slow to go fast with increasing momentum"?

Collective Expertise

Developing collective expertise within schools to achieve instructional coherence and precision of pedagogy is not a novel idea in education. But it's worth considering how this is best accomplished to have a sustainable impact on student learning growth. A vivid image from the past comes to mind in which a teacher, after 2 years of delivering instruction with fidelity using adopted curricular materials, is in tears because she is distraught by the fact that student growth has not been realized in her classroom. And yet in her mind she has instructional coherence and is attending to pedagogical precision. The lesson learned here is a key missing link; instructional coherence and precision of pedagogy are developed over time through *robust collaborative inquiry processes* that engage teams of teachers in collectively understanding how to improve the impact of teaching as learning unfolds among students within classrooms.

This brings into question the impact on student learning that is realized by *integrating curricular resources* (alignment of curriculum, instruction, and assessment), *creating instructional coherence* (a framework with guiding principles for high-quality teaching and learning), and *developing precision of pedagogy* (maximizing the impact on student learning by adjusting the interactions between the teacher and students and among students during the learning process). All three improvement strategies are essential, and yet, each requires specific expertise for improving the impact of teaching on student learning. However, as illustrated by the distraught teacher, we try to use instructional planning as if it were a silver bullet.

In the simplest form, developing collective expertise in schools occurs through the collaborative design and implementation of 3-week learning progressions with clearly defined learning tasks focused on a few key student success indicators. And when teacher teams co-lead robust collaborative inquiry processes to attend to this critical work, the result is greater instructional coherence with more precision of pedagogy. By design, improvement strategies that develop collective expertise have four essential components: 3-week learning progressions, clearly defined learning tasks, student success indicators, and a robust collaborative inquiry process.

The reason for structuring as 3-week instructional cycles is that when teaching is informed by evidence of learning within this timeframe, the potential impact is 20% annual growth in student learning (Marzano, 2006). From a practical standpoint, this would be akin to defining the learning targets and performance outcomes for 3-week units of study (learning progression) so that curricular resources, instructional strategies, and formative assessments are integrated to support the learning needs of all students. Attention is also directed to supporting all students in the successful completion of rigorous and complex learning tasks. As brilliantly concluded by Richard Elmore, "task predicts performance," and so the insights gained from 1- to 3-day student learning opportunities are rich sources of information for improving teaching and learning. Last, identifying a few key student success indicators ensures that student learning priorities stay in focus through the duration of the 3-week learning progression as students engage in multiday learning tasks. Student success indicators represent the transferrable skills that students develop over year-long timeframes, such as close and analytical reading, precise use of rigorous academic language, structured collaborative conversations, or evidence-based arguments and writing.

> Developing collective expertise in schools occurs through the collaborative design and implementation of 3-week learning progressions with clearly defined learning tasks focused on a few key student success indicators.

> *Developing collective expertise to deepen student learning calls upon teams of teachers to engage in robust collaborative inquiry processes that guide the design, implementation, and refinement of clearly delineated learning progressions with rigorous and complex learning tasks focused on a few key student success indicators.*

A few critical questions for consideration to develop collective expertise will be addressed in forthcoming chapters.

1. How should robust collaborative inquiry processes guide teacher teams to collectively design, implement, and refine learning progressions and classroom tasks?

2. How can curricular resources, instructional strategies, and formative assessments be integrated in a way that meets the learning needs of all students?

3. How can instructional coherence be shaped by a framework with guiding principles that promotes high-quality teaching and learning?

4. How should precision of pedagogy be developed by focusing attention on a few key student success indicators so that all students are able to apply these critical skills?

Continuous Improvement

The standards-based accountability movement in education has promoted the steadfast pursuit of evidence to monitor student progress and measure growth over time. This encompasses the analysis of annual summative assessments, trimester screening tools, quarterly interim assessments, monthly formative assessments, and daily checking for student understanding. The intended purpose of this assessment continuum is to inform the continuous improvement of student learning. But there is an inherent flaw in this theory of action that essentially states that analyzing evidence improves student learning. But are we monitoring and measuring the factors that most influence student learning? The reality is that *improvement of practice precedes growth in student learning*, and therefore the focus should be knowing and understanding the impact of teaching on student learning to realize the desired growth in student learning results.

To this end, knowing the impact on student learning should move away from analyzing student learning outcomes toward clarifying the pedagogical practices that will have the most impact on improving learning for all students. *Knowing the impact on student learning* would then shift to predicting the impact of teaching on student learning with a clearly defined theory of action for achieving the desired growth in student learning. The most critical question may be: "What is the desired growth in student learning, and how will we know the impact of pedagogical practices as students progress toward realizing this outcome?" This builds a strong foundation for guiding continuous improvement because it focuses the collective efforts of teachers and site leaders on seeking evidence of impact on "learning progress" rather than monitoring and measuring "learning outcomes."

Inevitably, improvement efforts will come to identify the *problems of practice* that are impeding growth in student learning within and among classrooms. Understanding the root causes of these barriers to learning is essential and requires that teachers and site leaders seek solutions through collaborative inquiry. Such efforts focus on both challenges observed among students during the learning process as well as challenges teachers experience while engaging students in learning tasks. This takes shape in the form of asking probing questions such as "What could be the cause of . . .", "I wonder how to . . .", and "What would be the impact if . . ." It's as simple as first understanding the cause, followed by identifying viable solutions, and then considering the effect on improving student learning.

Overcoming problems of practice to improve teaching and learning is an ongoing and never-ending process. Sustaining these efforts requires that schools adopt a mindset and structured process for *continuously improving through disciplined inquiry*. The four phases of a collaborative inquiry process begin with analyzing evidence to clearly define the problems of practice. Then comes designing a theory of action for improving teaching and learning with evidence to know the impact on student learning growth followed by implementing action steps and making adjustments along the way informed by the evidence of impact. And last is reflecting on what worked best, why, and how to develop shared depth and understanding of the most promising practices for achieving growth in student learning. The collaborative inquiry cycle can serve as a school-wide improvement process if evidence of learning is shared by each teacher team at the conclusion of each 3-week inquiry cycle. This affords site leaders and teachers the opportunity to engage in a robust collaborative inquiry process every

Knowing the impact on student learning should move away from analyzing student learning outcomes toward clarifying the pedagogical practices that will have the most impact on improving learning for all students.

6 weeks for the purpose of overcoming common problems of practice and the sharing of promising practices.

> *Achieving growth in student learning requires that schools adopt a continuous improvement process for analyzing evidence to clearly define problems of practice, designing theories of action that improve teaching and learning, and knowing the impact on student learning to refine improvement efforts and identify promising practices.*

A few critical questions for consideration to guide continuous improvement will be addressed in forthcoming chapters.

1. How can evidence of impact on student learning guide the design, implementation, and refinement of practices to achieve equitable growth in student learning?

2. How can monitoring of student learning progress focus on seeking evidence of impact to know the extent to which improvement efforts are achieving equitable growth in student learning?

3. How should improvement efforts be shaped by recurring collaborative inquiry cycles for the purpose of overcoming problems of practice and the sharing of promising practices?

Setting the Stage

School districts that successfully create a coherent system of continuous improvement have a common vision with guiding principles (clarity of focus, shared leadership, collective expertise, and continuous improvement) for co-constructing the most critical work in collaboration with school sites. It is important to note that navigating systemic improvement requires a collaborative inquiry mindset and structured process for co-leading efforts to achieve equitable growth in student learning. The following is how Anywhere School District began the journey of becoming a *District on the Move* and how one school within the district, Somewhere School, assisted with initiating and sustaining systemic improvement through the ongoing efforts to become a *School on the Move*.

At the onset of the school year, Anywhere School District established a focus on literacy and critical thinking skills to guide school sites with improving student learning outcomes. This priority stemmed from the analysis of multiple measures and review of classroom observations that pointed to the fact that many students struggled with completing rigorous and complex learning tasks. The root causes of these student inequities were found to be gaps in close and analytical reading skills and the ability to analyze, interpret, evaluate, problem solve, and justify with evidence. Each school was asked to create an action plan for implementing these priorities. At an upcoming principal meeting, these action plans were to be shared and discussed among principals and district leaders. The principal of Somewhere School, Jacob Westfall, had spent several weeks collaborating with staff to create the action plan and was looking forward to an opportunity to learn how other schools were attending to this critical work.

Erin McFarland, assistant superintendent of education services, had been tasked with coordinating the principal meeting. Much time and attention was dedicated to organizing key topics and ensuring there were opportunities for sharing and asking questions. She was dismayed when the principals voiced more questions than answers as to how best to support students and staff with moving forward the district priorities of literacy and critical thinking. The site action plans were vague, with little clarity as to how strategies would be implemented or how evidence would be monitored to know the impact on student learning. It was clear principals wanted more guidance, and so a list of key questions were created to go deeper with designing more precise, actionable, and impactful plans.

1. What are the school-wide priorities for student learning?

2. What measures of student progress or growth will define our success?

3. Which student success indicators (cognitive skills and application of key concepts) will best inform the design of student tasks and learning progressions?

(Continued)

(Continued)

4. Which high-yield pedagogical practices will have the greatest impact on student learning?

5. How will evidence of learning inform both timely student feedback and adjustments of student learning supports?

6. What timeframes should guide our collective efforts with engaging students in short cycles of instruction and improving upon teaching and learning practices?

Erin asked Jacob to stay after the principal meeting to debrief because they had worked on other committees in the past and had a good working relationship. As they reflected on their observations and insights, themes emerged as to how principals had framed the work with their staffs. The four descriptors were compliant, rogue, fragmented, and focused. Some principals were asking exactly what was wanted from the district in their action plans, whereas others wanted full autonomy to design what was best for their schools. Others seemed to be torn on what to do because there were many competing priorities among staff, and a few schools already had staff consensus as to how best to support the district priorities. Erin was uncertain how to proceed with such divergence among principals and variation in school action plans.

Jacob offered to assist by forming a small work group with a few principals, and Erin asked if this group could be representative of the four themes from their meeting (compliant, rogue, fragmented, and focused) because this would provide insights needed to support each type of school. In the end, it was decided that visiting each school site together would be most beneficial. This would allow Jacob an opportunity to discuss the work with each principal and talk with the school staff to garner takeaways that could assist his school. And Erin could learn more about each school site and how they were understanding and attending to the work at hand. A simple diagram was created for capturing insights from each school visit that noted what was believed to be the key drivers for shaping the work at hand: clarity of focus, shared leadership, collective expertise, and continuous improvement. Jacob would follow up with Erin as to which schools would be visited and a schedule of dates and times that were preferred by the school sites.

Anywhere School District is not unique from the perspective of how schools and districts engage in the process of shaping culture, developing capacity, and creating coherence. Are there similarities to your own school or district? What insights or key takeaways can be gleaned from the beginning journey of Anywhere School District and its school sites? What would you do next if you were Erin and Jacob? In the forthcoming chapter we will dive into the first key driver of school improvement: clarity of focus. What will unfold is how schools and districts create a strategic focus for achieving equitable student growth with clearly delineated improvement strategies guided by short cycles of collaborative inquiry.

Creating Clarity of Focus 2

Educators have the power to positively transform the lives of students. To do so requires clarity of focus so that improvement efforts overcome the root causes of student equity issues. Closing the achievement and opportunity gaps that exist within our schools is a foundational civil rights issue in the United States, and school systems that place equity at the heart of every decision are *student centered* rather than focused on the needs of adults. Now, more than ever, it is essential for educators to use this equity lens for defining what to do and, more importantly, why to do it. To have a more perfect union, it is imperative that we continually ask whether the decisions made in classrooms, school buildings, and board rooms will overcome or reinforce the prevailing student inequities.

To this point, Chris, when serving as superintendent of the Long Beach, would be asked two questions on a regular basis: "What was the 'North Star' that kept him and the district grounded in the work at hand?" and "What was the secret to the success of Long Beach in closing student achievement and opportunity gaps?" Every time the answer was that each classroom needed to be good enough for our own children and that all schools embraced the Long Beach mission statement of *supporting the personal and intellectual success of every student every day*. If these belief statements became the driving force of all educators in their daily work, then all students would be prepared for the college and career of their choice. Clarity of focus exists only if in fact there exists a common purpose and agreed-upon outcomes that guide the daily work of teachers and leaders within and among school sites.

To bring the Long Beach mission statement to fruition required a set of goals and objectives grounded in achieving equitable outcomes for all students. A strategic plan was developed with input from all

Clarity of focus exists only if in fact there exists a common purpose and agreed-upon outcomes that guide the daily work of teachers and leaders within and among school sites.

stakeholders to create a collective commitment among students, parents, staff, higher education partners, and business leaders. This aspirational vision focused district efforts on addressing the closure of student achievement and opportunity gaps within all Long Beach schools. To ensure the strategic plan was treated as a living document, there were ongoing modifications based on recurring data and emerging problems of practice as well as a comprehensive update every 5 years. This was critical for focusing direction of the system and creating internal accountability for equitable growth in student learning as defined by the following goals:

> **Goal 1:** *Ensure equitable opportunities for every student.*
>
> **Goal 2:** *Provide a safe, welcoming, respectful, and rigorous learning environment for every member of the school community.*
>
> **Goal 3:** *Promote academic growth for every student.*
>
> **Goal 4:** *Establish college and career readiness for every student.*
>
> **Goal 5:** *Support effective communication throughout the district.*

A strategic plan developed by all stakeholders won't realize a more equitable learning experience for students. In other words, clarity of focus is not enough, and there needs to be a way to enact an agreed-upon purpose and common outcomes for student learning. To enhance and personalize the learning experiences of students, staff, and parents, a process must be employed that develops collective efficacy through collaborative inquiry. This process needs to be equity driven, leverage the expertise among school sites and district personnel, focus on the academic and social-emotional needs of students, and be grounded in continuous improvement cycles with clear next steps moving forward. And teachers, site staff, and school administrators have to be supported by district leaders to become equity warriors who can effectively do this difficult work.

To this end, Long Beach developed the collaborative inquiry visit (CIV) that engaged teachers, support staff, and administrators to be the driving force for enhancing student learning. The CIV process paired schools with similar problems of practice to visit each other's sites three times a year for classroom observations and review of formative and summative data that clarified next steps for closing student achievement and opportunity gaps. At the high school level, the CIVs also included *quarterly visits* to assist with ensuring all students were college and career ready upon graduation based on the outcomes in the LBUSD graduate profile denoted in Figure 2.1. School sites routinely reviewed the graduate profile to identify areas of student growth and progress toward demonstrating these skill sets. This ensured that the CIVs were connected to common criteria of student success.

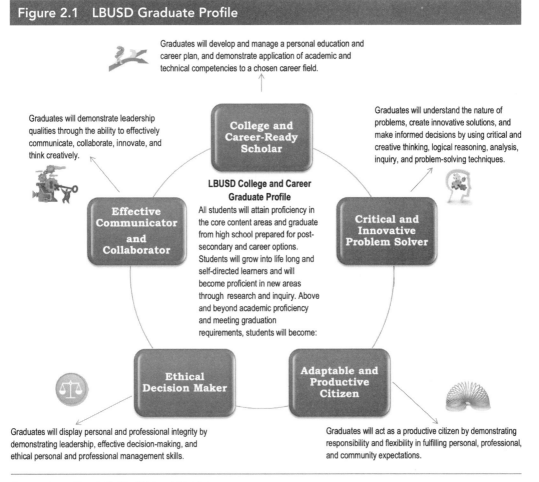

Figure 2.1   LBUSD Graduate Profile

Graduates will develop and manage a personal education and career plan, and demonstrate application of academic and technical competencies to a chosen career field.

Graduates will demonstrate leadership qualities through the ability to effectively communicate, collaborate, innovate, and think creatively.

Graduates will understand the nature of problems, create innovative solutions, and make informed decisions by using critical and creative thinking, logical reasoning, analysis, inquiry, and problem-solving techniques.

College and Career-Ready Scholar

Effective Communicator and Collaborator

Critical and Innovative Problem Solver

LBUSD College and Career Graduate Profile

All students will attain proficiency in the core content areas and graduate from high school prepared for post-secondary and career options. Students will grow into life long and self-directed learners and will become proficient in new areas through research and inquiry. Above and beyond academic proficiency and meeting graduation requirements, students will become:

Ethical Decision Maker

Adaptable and Productive Citizen

Graduates will display personal and professional integrity by demonstrating leadership, effective decision-making, and ethical personal and professional management skills.

Graduates will act as a productive citizen by demonstrating responsibility and flexibility in fulfilling personal, professional, and community expectations.

Source: Long Beach Unified School District.

During these 3- to 4-hour quarterly visits, department heads, members of the school instructional leadership team (ILT), school administrators, and student leaders met with the superintendent and other central office administrators to review formative and summative data in relation to school progress. The student attributes within the LBUSD graduate profile were used to bring clarity as to whether all students were demonstrating progress and personal growth toward achieving these critical skill sets. Both the CIV and quarterly visit processes were built upon an equity model that focused on closing achievement and opportunity gaps through the shared leadership of all participants. These continuous improvement cycles were a time to collaboratively address problems of practice, identify best practices, and clarify next steps for moving forward the most critical work of each school site.

The Long Beach schools truly became laboratories of innovation focused on how best to meet the academic and social-emotional needs of all students. And because there were clear next steps to be taken before the next visit, everyone felt accountable to attend to areas of improvement, student interventions, and staff professional learning. School sites took ownership of the individualized learning needs of students and staff in a more professional manner than if the central office had mandated how to address improvement efforts. And because central office leaders participated as valued members of these continuous improvement cycles, the Long Beach system was better positioned to support school improvement efforts in the quest for excellence for all students.

The purpose of sharing this example is to frame a critical question: "How do school leaders and teachers create clarity of focus that guides the ongoing process of improving practices and student learning outcomes?" We know that when school sites collectively define the desired impact of teaching on student learning at the classroom desk, a coherent path of school improvement emerges that gradually results in achieving site and district goals for student learning growth (Westover, 2019). But this path of progress varies among schools within a school district, and understanding the causes of this variance in focusing school improvement efforts is critical for realizing growth in learning for all students. We have gained many insights over the past two decades and now understand the level of influence on focusing direction that is caused by the variability of school climate, culture, capacity, and coherence within and among school sites. Clarity of focus cannot be created without attending to these root causes of variance and overcoming the inherent problems of practice.

Problems of Practice
and Promising Practices

Have you ever attended a professional learning venue wherein a school or district leader presented a visual, told a success story, or shared a resource that moved participants to take action by replicating what was learned? I call this the "beacon of light" method, which instills a false sense of hope that success can be achieved by following the same steps as others. What most don't realize is that to fully understand how these leaders achieved their success requires a deeper analysis of the changes in climate, culture, capacity, and coherence that took place over time. Climate is how you feel about the work, whereas culture is how you take action. Capacity is confidence in your ability to do the work, whereas coherence is a shared depth of understanding that creates meaning for doing the work. And although those attending the professional learning venue may have a positive attitude and a desire to take action, there will certainly be dissonance when shared with school staff not in attendance. The greatest challenge with creating clarity of focus is that it cannot be attained by learning from others, rather it requires a collaborative inquiry process that engages school staff in collectively defining the most critical work at hand.

> Clarity of focus requires a collaborative inquiry process that engages school staff in collectively defining the most critical work at hand.

This begins to illustrate the problems of practice that occur among school sites in their efforts to create clarity of focus. Three general categories frame the challenges most often experienced among school leaders and teachers: compliance, prescription, and fragmentation. When setting direction to move forward as a school site, there can be a compliance orientation caused by groupthink or what is known as a herd mentality. This occurs when there is acceptance of or conformity with the majority viewpoint, such as when schools simply comply with district goals or student learning priorities without much criticality or forethought. In reality it is safer and easier to conform than it is to question the validity of an already established vision. The common phrase "Don't rock the boat" comes to mind when considering why this tendency is often seen among school leaders or teachers who don't want to be seen as a disrupter or outlier.

In sharp contrast, prescription can become the mode of operation when school sites have strong convictions for a predefined path moving forward. The prevailing desire to have command and control of both the school focus and action steps promotes an authoritative, top-down approach to focusing direction. Fine-grained details are micro-managed in an effort to ensure the already known path moving forward is followed by all without any distractions to get off course. We would call this a "fall-in-line" mentality that can breed dissent and resentment among school staff.

If compliance is conformity, and prescription is control, then fragmentation is "everyone for themselves." At face value, a fragmented school appears to be moving in a unified direction, but the reality is that behind the scenes there are ulterior motives and hidden agendas.

These are seen as factions of staff members play along to get along but are actually protecting their own interests. There is a distinction between words and actions. In a fragmented school there is a sense that we're in this together based on words, but when observing behaviors and actions, another story is playing out. This would be akin to the adage of protecting the status quo and resisting a change in focus or direction that is in contrast to individual beliefs and values.

To circumvent these prevailing problems of practices, there are more promising practices that schools can consider for creating clarity of focus. Michael Fullan has noted that focusing direction is a key driver for coherence making: shared depth of understanding about the nature of the work and how it affects the results desired for student achievement (Fullan & Kirtman, 2019). To reframe these insights, promising practices focus the collective efforts of school leaders and teachers with clearly defining the work with the greatest potential for achieving equitable growth in student learning. The key phrase here is "collective efforts clearly define the work that will maximize the impact on student learning." Schools that engage in collaborative inquiry informed by the following key questions will be more successful with shaping a common vision and structured process for co-leading improvement efforts.

1. How can a *moral imperative for improving student learning* be shaped as staff share personal experiences, beliefs, and values in defining the most critical work for the school?

2. How can staff input and feedback establish agreed-upon *structures and processes for collaborative decision-making* that will inform school-wide priorities and action steps?

3. How can staff engage in authentic and vulnerable conversations about *confidence in the ability of individuals and teams* to successfully implement school improvement efforts?

4. How can staff come to recognize that *creating shared meaning and depth of understanding for the work at hand* is an ongoing process wherein the school continuously adapts and adjusts to meet the learning needs of all students?

These four questions have been garnered over many years working with schools that have demonstrated consistent forward motion and high levels of staff engagement in creating clarity of focus. There is a stark difference between consistent forward motion with clarity of focus versus the previously noted challenges experienced by schools that have gone down the path of compliance, prescription, or fragmentation. What should stand out most from these guiding questions is the collaborative inquiry stance taken by school leaders and teachers in the collective pursuit of achieving equitable growth in student learning. What matters most for schools is not defining goals or priorities for student achievement but rather collectively shaping a shared vision and action steps to realize success for all students.

District and School Story

A week had passed since district leaders and school principals of Anywhere School District convened to share site action plans focused on the district priorities of literacy and critical thinking. Jacob Westfall, principal of Somewhere School, had been able to schedule follow-up meetings with a few principals to discuss improvement strategies in more detail. His primary purpose was to gain insights that could assist him with coordinating next steps with his staff. Erin McFarland had agreed to join Jacob on these visits, and she was eager to understand how each school was taking action to improve the agreed-upon student learning priorities. They had determined it was best to visit schools based on the four themes observed during the principal meeting" compliant, rogue, fragmented, and focused.

First up was the school led by the newest principal in the district that fit into the compliant category. Upon entering the school it was clear that the school was fully aligned with the district goals and priorities because the office was decorated with visuals depicting the district vision. In fact, the principal was sure to bring this to Erin's attention so that she saw his solidarity for the common good. Most of the conversations about the school action plan circled back to whether it met the expectations of the district. This thinking became even more evident when teachers passing by were asked about the school action plan. There was an overwhelming response from school staff that referred to district priorities with little mention of school site needs. There was almost a sense of comfort among staff that a focus for student learning was already defined, and many had asked Erin about the next steps moving

(Continued)

(Continued)

forward. Upon leaving the school both Jacob and Erin had the
same sense that the school had gladly conformed to district
expectations but that there was an unhealthy reliance on the
district for defining next steps without much consideration for
learning needs of students at the school site. The calm and
relaxed atmosphere almost felt apathetic and without a sense
of passion or desire to improve.

The next school was led by the most senior principal in the
district, who fit into the rogue category. The visit almost felt
fully planned out as Erin and Jacob were greeted by the office
staff with an offering of water and snacks, and the conference
room for the meeting was boldly branded with school accolades,
recognitions, and press releases. Upon entering the conference
room, the principal subtly pointed out several of the awards
that she was most proud of receiving. The meeting started out
oddly because the principal did not seem to know the purpose
and quickly began to note the ongoing great work of the staff
with little mention of the district priorities of literacy and critical
thinking. When Jacob inquired as to how these priorities were
being addressed, the principal's response was framed in how
the school was further along, had already addressed these
areas, and was now moving into a different phase of work. The
staff also expressed their work with a similar sense of arrogance
and overconfidence that mostly related back to the numerous
accolades from the community. Erin wondered if the school had
done a deep dive into evidence of student literacy and critical
thinking skills. It seemed that school autonomy and identity were
more important than student learning needs.

Before arriving at the third school site, Jacob and Erin had a brief
conversation about the principal being the third site administrator
in the last 5 years to lead the school. The staff was difficult to
manage. This was the primary reason the school had been labeled
as fragmented. After sitting in the lobby for 15 minutes, the
principal showed up apologizing that an unexpected emergency
had come up. When pressed by Erin, the principal shared that the
staff was not happy with the tardy policy, and so the administrative
team was ensuring that all students entered classrooms on
time. This was taking up quite a bit of administrators' time

as they escorted tardy students into their classrooms, not to mention dealing with discipline follow-up for students who were consistently tardy. Jacob inquired as to the role of staff in reducing student tardiness, and the principal's coy response was simply that it was mixed and varied. As the conversation shifted to the site action plan, the theme of "mixed and varied" continued because the priorities of literacy and critical thinking were not equally embraced by staff with divergent thinking among departments. Although there was recognition that students lacked literacy and critical thinking skills, there were different opinions as to whether these priorities applied to all teachers and each department. Literacy was seen by many staff as the role of English teachers. And critical thinking was embraced by honors teachers but was not by those who taught regular classes. Rather than creating an action plan for the school, it appeared that the more important conversation among staff was whether all felt it was their responsibility to support student literacy and critical thinking. The meeting ended with the principal asking Erin and Jacob for feedback and ideas on how to move the school forward as a collective; it seemed that every time there was agreement on what to do, there was a lack of action among the staff. It felt to the principal that this disunity provided many staff with a reason not to move forward with improving student learning. Jacob's only comment to the principal was that there clearly was more happening behind the scenes than was known by the principal.

The last principal to be visited had come from outside the district 2 years ago and seemed to lead from behind the scenes. Erin had not remembered visiting the school last year, and although Jacob knew the principal, he had not had any conversations that would give him a pulse on the progress of the school. But the principal's action plan was well designed and had clear and focused action steps. The principal was waiting outside of the school and offered to walk classrooms with Erin and Jacob before meeting in the conference room. Teachers were open to pausing instruction, talking about what students were doing and responding to questions. The theme of literacy and critical thinking was evident, and although there were different ideas among teachers, there were many consistencies with instructional

(Continued)

(Continued)

strategies and student supports. Upon entering the conference room, the principal shared copies of the site action plan and noted that she thought that walking classrooms and talking to teachers would be more beneficial. Erin, being skeptical, asked whether the teachers knew about the visit. The principal said no and that teachers' willingness to share their work was because they had become comfortable with classroom walkthroughs and sharing ideas during staff meetings. Jacob asked how the school action plan was created and was surprised to learn that a core group of teachers had been given release time to write the plan, share the draft with staff, and finalize the plan based on feedback. What stood out most to Jacob and Erin was that the principal, upon arriving at the school 2 years ago, told the staff that her goal was to develop the expertise among teachers in the school so that when she eventually left, the school would be stronger than when she arrived. It appeared that the staff had taken her comments to heart and were comfortable leading the work with her support.

Jacob's school was close by for a short debriefing of what was learned from each school. On the conference room whiteboard was already written the titles of conformity, rogue, fragmented, and focused. Erin erased the word "focused" and wrote the word "coherent" in its place, noting that the last school was not only focused but had coherence among the staff. And Jacob erased the word "rogue" and wrote the word "prescriptive" because his feeling was that the principal and the teachers spoken to were rigid in thinking and uncompromising in beliefs and actions. Erin emphasized the need to capture insights to help her think through how to support divergent schools to move the work forward, whereas Jacob noted that he wanted to identify what was behind the climate and culture of the schools visited. Erin wrote an essential question on the whiteboard: "What aspects of school climate and culture most affect schools with defining student learning priorities and moving the work forward?" After an hour of dialog and charting ideas, the chart in Figure 2.2 was written on the whiteboard. Each took a picture of the chart and agreed to meet again after further analyzing and making sense of the information.

Figure 2.2 Key Indicators of School Climate and Culture				
ARCHETYPE	**CLIMATE**	**CULTURE**	**IMPACT**	**QUESTIONS**
Compliant	A desire to be seen as supporting the vision set forth by the school district	Wanting guidance from the district to plan action steps moving forward	Lack of urgency to change practices and improve student learning	Why is the school not seeking their own solutions based on student learning needs?
Prescriptive	A strong belief that the school knows what to do, how to do it, and does not need any support	A rigid mindset and lack of openness to deviate from the predefined school plan and actions	Overconfidence in action steps due to the inability or unwillingness to question thinking	What evidence does the school have that validates they are on track?
Fragmented	A lack of unity stemming from individuals wanting to maintain their sense of autonomy	Bringing forth problems that prevent staff from making decisions to move forward	Protecting the status quo, which has allowed staff to be independent with their work	Why does the staff resist working together to learn how to improve student learning?
Coherent	A feeling of staff empowerment for making decisions that guide school improvements	A willingness to work together, share ideas, and learn from others	An inquiry process led by staff that promotes informed decision-making	What led staff to embrace a culture of collaboration and co-learning?

© 2022 InnovateEd

Creating a Strategic Focus for Equitable Student Growth

The story of Anywhere School District and Somewhere School may resonate with educators as the themes of compliance, prescription, fragmentation, and coherence certainly exist among schools within every district. Without a structured process for clarifying student learning priorities, school climate and culture can circumvent efforts of site leaders and teachers to focus direction. Shifting the questions listed in Figure 2.2 into statements brings forth the underlying conditions needed to move schools forward. These core tenets can assist schools with shaping a common mindset and structured process for creating clarity of focus.

- Seek to understand the learning needs of all students in every classroom.

- Identify viable sources of student learning evidence for informed decision-making.

- Work together to overcome the most common challenges of teaching and learning.

- Engage in agile co-learning and productive collaboration to promote collaborative inquiry.

Richard Elmore coined a famous phrase that has greatly influenced how we have come to know the impact of teaching on student learning; task predicts performance (City et al., 2009). The implication is that understanding student learning needs is best achieved through close examination of learning tasks at the student desk. Although there is value in analyzing student progress and performance on interim and annual assessments, these measures do not represent the authentic learning experiences that play out as students engage in learning within classrooms. If student learning challenges are to be resolved, adjustments need to affect how students engage in rigorous and complex tasks as part of daily instruction. The focus of improvement efforts should be where teaching and learning challenges originate: at the student desk.

If task predicts student performance, then what are the indicators of student learning? In *Districts on the Move* we described "visible evidence of student learning" as the key cognitive strategies for students to apply content knowledge. The intent was to shift the indicators of learning from students *showing what they know* to students *demonstrating what they can do*. Higher-order thinking, close and analytical reading, precise use of rigorous academic language, evidence-based arguments, structured collaborative conversations, and evidence-based writing are the transferable skills that make learning visible. A critical question for consideration is: "Which key cognitive skills are most essential for students to successfully complete rigorous and complex learning tasks?" By asking this question, the collaborative inquiry process of prioritizing student learning needs becomes more focused on the indicators of student success. The specificity and precision that accompany the analysis of student learning tasks result in a deeper understanding of the strengths and constraints among students as learning unfolds at the classroom desk.

A critical step for clarifying student learning needs is to understand the relationship between lag outcomes, lead metrics, and student success indicators. Lag outcomes are annual measures of student performance, whereas lead metrics are quarterly or trimester assessments that monitor student growth in relation to the lag outcome. And student success indicators are the key cognitive skills that students apply when completing rigorous and complex tasks within a specific learning progression. In this way, students apply close and analytical reading skills to complete learning tasks as part of 3-week learning progressions. The improvement of student literacy skills is monitored by an interim assessment at the conclusion of 9 to 12 weeks. At year-end, a summative assessment measures the annual growth of student literacy skills.

To put these sources of learning evidence into context, consider how a coach would provide feedback to an athlete while standing on the finish line of a 100-yard dash, 5K run, or marathon. Under which scenario would insights best be gained to inform that athlete of key improvements? Clearly the shorter distance allows for more precise observations and more specific feedback. This analogy is validated by the research of Robert Marzano (2006) in *Classroom Assessment and Grading that Work*, which noted a significant difference in effect size with improving student learning from reviewing classroom learning tasks (.80) versus analyzing summative assessments (.34).

Let's come full circle as to how schools can clarify the common problems of practice among students that are barriers to realizing equitable growth in learning; establish guiding principles that promote a climate of co-learning and culture of collaborative inquiry; seek to understand the challenges that students experience when completing rigorous and complex tasks in classrooms by focusing on student success indicators—key cognitive strategies for applying content knowledge—make clear linkages among learning tasks, lead metrics, and lag outcomes to develop shared understanding as to how "task predicts performance"; and adopt a root cause analysis process that closely analyzes student learning strengths and constraints to clearly define the focus of school-wide improvement efforts.

Clearly Delineating Improvement Strategies

Creating clarity of focus would be analogous to spotting an iceberg floating in the distance and then discerning how best to navigate a course moving forward. The location of the iceberg is known; however, there is much uncertainty as to its size and shape with 90% of the iceberg's volume looming beneath the waterline. The implication is that having clarity of focus is the faint starting point for clearly delineating improvement strategies that guide the collective efforts of school leaders and teachers. Clarity of focus can create a false sense of confidence because school priorities can be seen as a beacon of light for navigating a path moving forward. This would be akin to establishing literacy as a school priority that focuses efforts on improving close and analytical reading skills of all students. The "what" is clear, whereas the "how" is uncertain. This sounds a lot like the iceberg has been spotted, but there is no certainty with navigating the path ahead.

The key to moving forward is understanding the causal pathway that links school priorities with student success indicators, high-yield instructional practices, and evidence of student learning to clearly delineate improvement strategies. This takes the form of a school implementation plan that clearly delineates the action steps for moving forward school-wide improvement efforts. Six key questions guide the collective efforts of site leaders and teachers.

1. What are the school-wide priorities and desired growth for student learning?

2. Which student success indicators will best inform the design of student tasks and learning progressions?

3. Which high-yield pedagogical practices will have the greatest impact on improving learning for all students?

> The key to moving forward is understanding the causal pathway that links school priorities with student success indicators, high-yield instructional practices, and evidence of learning to clearly delineate improvement strategies.

4. How will evidence of learning inform both timely student feedback and adjustments of student learning supports?

5. What structures, processes, and supports are needed to develop collective expertise through agile co-learning and productive collaboration?

6. What timeframes should guide our collective efforts with engaging students in short cycles of instruction and improving upon teaching and learning practices?

Each of these questions will take a school down a path of inquiry as the strengths and constraints inherent to school climate, culture, capacity, and coherence will be brought to the surface. In using these questions over the past several years to assist school districts with strategically planning and leading improvement efforts, variances that exist within and among schools are always revealed. For example, in some school districts the concept of student success indicators and high-yield pedagogical practices are not openly discussed, which raises concerns among district and site leaders that a shared depth of understanding does not exist among school staff. This implies a lack of coherence within and among schools in the district. In addition, not all schools have a climate of co-learning or a collaborative culture that is foundational for robust and productive conversations. And the varying capacity among school staff for engaging students in high-quality teaching and learning is perceived as a barrier for achieving consensus with what to do and how to do it. But aren't these the exact reasons why schools should collectively seek answers to these questions and clearly delineate improvement strategies to move the work forward together? We can draw the conclusion that school districts assess readiness for leading improvement efforts based on the state of school climate, culture, capacity, and coherence. This "current state" thinking can promote the prevalence of the status quo and resistance to change moving forward that is based on the premise of waiting for the right conditions before engaging in improvement efforts when in reality the path moving forward is dependent upon shaping a common mindset and establishing a structured process for collaborative decision-making. School leaders and teachers who approach leading improvement efforts through a collaborative inquiry stance will be more successful with navigating the complexities of transforming climate, developing culture, building capacity, and creating coherence.

Guiding Short Cycles
of Collaborative Inquiry

A phenomenon called "goal displacement" has been described by Fullan (2015) wherein the process of developing capacity and commitment for improving student learning becomes displaced by creating a plan for taking action. In other words, completing the plan becomes the goal in and of itself. A reason for this displacement is that school plans are often perceived as static, yearlong, and not to be deviated from once finalized. This is further exasperated by the fact that plans are often not written for the school but to comply with external requirements of the district office or to meet state-level mandates. And once written, the likelihood is very low that school plans will serve as a guide for site improvement efforts.

A shift in mindset is needed from that of creating a yearlong plan to clearly delineating action steps that guide improvement efforts for 9 to 12 weeks. This implies that at the conclusion of each time period, school leaders and teachers reflect on progress and impact, refine improvement strategies, and move forward with more clarity for achieving growth in student learning. And most importantly, this iterative approach promotes a collaborative inquiry process because there is an emphasis on taking action to learn what most affects student learning, understand how and why it works, and share key insights to inform the actions of others moving forward. Such an approach requires schools to "pivot" every 9 to 12 weeks, which is significantly different than maintaining the same focus for the school year. Essentially it forces schools to embrace change and lead an agile improvement process.

The shift from creating a yearlong plan with annual goals for growth in student learning to that of guiding an agile improvement process with short cycles of collaborative inquiry can be a challenging task for schools and districts alike. This relates back to the prevailing conditions of compliance, prescription, and fragmentation. There is a tendency to provide school sites with planning templates to be completed in a prescribed manner, which are intended to serve as a guide for yearlong improvement efforts. The problem is that a yearlong plan created for the purpose of compliance and completed in a regimented manner does not create ownership or internal accountability for the work at hand. In contrast, action plans that extend over a 9- to 12-week period have more precision and specificity and require monitoring of progress and assessing impact to refine action steps for the next inquiry cycle. Simple, short improvement cycles can best be considered to be "learning cycles." In the same manner that classroom teachers adapt and adjust instructional strategies daily and weekly to better meet the learning needs of students when teaching a 3-week unit of study, school sites should reframe the work as 9- to 12-week improvement cycles that require adjustments in real time and carry forward lessons learned. In doing so, with each short cycle of collaborative inquiry, the school site creates more clarity, develops more precision, and improves capacity to achieve equitable growth in student learning.

The Path of Progress for Foothill Elementary School

Foothill Elementary School located in Corona, California, is one of 29 elementary schools within Corona-Norco USD. The school serves a student population of 40% socioeconomic disadvantaged, 13% English learners, and 20% special education students. Foothill Elementary began its journey toward becoming a school on the move in 2017 at a time when site-level improvement efforts were being leveraged to shape district-wide coherence. Over a 3-year period, the Foothill staff of 35 teachers and two site administrators demonstrated a resilient commitment to creating clarity of focus, cultivating shared leadership, developing collective expertise, and leading continuous improvement.

At the onset, the school could be described as fragmented yet having a collaborative culture and a collective commitment to improve learning for all students. In retrospect, Foothill would fall into the category of believers because there was a positive climate and culture; however, the school lacked the collective capacity to navigate the ongoing process of creating coherence. Dr. Joni Howard, having been principal at Foothill for 3 years, knew that the staff was ready to move forward together and needed a structured process to guide their collective efforts. The initial approach was to develop the school into a professional learning community. It was evident though that the staff perceived this as a structural change with predefined steps rather than a robust capacity-building strategy. In moving forward, the strength of the school climate and culture would need to be leveraged to focus improvement efforts on developing capacity and creating coherence.

The emphasis during the 2017–2018 school year was focusing direction of school improvement efforts by engaging in collaborative inquiry.

A team of teachers representing each grade level convened with site administrators to co-design a school implementation plan, and through this inquiry process, the root causes of teaching and learning challenges were identified. The staff had been struggling with understanding best use of a new ELA adoption and the integration of multiple assessment tools to guide recurring cycles of instruction. In effect, teachers were shifting instruction to align with curricular resources and student assessments rather than focusing efforts on a few learning priorities and key student success indicators. To focus school improvement efforts, the following was initially adopted by the school to receive input and feedback from grade-level teams and move forward based on a collective vision of student success.

School Focus: Equip all students to effectively communicate and collaborate by analyzing, problem-solving, reasoning, justifying, and critiquing others using rigorous and precise content area academic language.

Student Success Indicators: Access, interpret, and analyze grade-level content; communicate and justify with evidence; collaborate in pairs or groups to problem solve and critique the reasoning of others.

Instructional Strategies: Model and scaffold close reading of grade-level texts; use sentence and conversation starters to support arguments with evidence; model strategies for effective pair and group work for successful completion of tasks that require justifying, reasoning, and critiquing others with evidence.

By the end of the first year, the staff began to realize that improvement efforts were more impactful when 3- to 4-week instructional cycles were guided by a school focus, student success indicators, and high-yield instructional strategies. And as teacher teams reflected on student progress and key learnings at the conclusion of each instructional cycle, this structured process for informed decision-making was developing the confidence and capacity of teachers to improve student learning. Rather than focusing efforts on planning effective use of curricular resources and assessment tools, the school was shifting to developing precision of pedagogy based on evidence of impact on student learning growth. At this point in time, the principal offered to expand the team to include two members from each grade level so that structured time could be provided for deeper collaborative inquiry. The result was a commitment from each grade-level pair to serve as lead learners, help shape school improvement efforts, and support grade-level collaborative inquiry processes.

As the work progressed into the 2018–2019 school year, the momentum created by the teacher leaders guiding improvement efforts allowed for candid feedback as to the progress of each grade level. This led to a deeper root cause analysis process to discern the problems of practice among students that were preventing growth in learning for all students. The emphasis on close reading of grade-level information brought to the forefront that the analysis of student writing would provide better insights into student learning needs. Grade-level teams agreed to analyze student writing products at the conclusion of 3- to 4-week instructional cycles. The teams identified several school-wide trends and patterns in their feedback: students struggled when completing rigorous and complex tasks in pairs or groups because there was too much reliance on teacher modeling and direct instruction; students were not able to use evidence effectively when justifying, reasoning, or supporting thinking; and students were not writing coherent paragraphs that clearly communicated a response to a claim. The staff recognized that overcoming these student skill gaps would require stronger vertical articulation and adoption of a formal 4-week collaborative inquiry cycle focused on improving teaching and learning. As the year progressed, one teacher's comment was insightful: "I assumed that the school focus and student success indicators would remain consistent all year, but we continue to refine our instructional priorities, teaching practices, and student supports. At first I was frustrated by these ongoing adjustments and then realized that we are continuously updating our school implementation plan to better meet the learning needs of all students."

Sustainability is the true test of improvement efforts primarily because school climate and culture are in a constant state of flux as staff beliefs, attitudes, and behaviors change in relation to the work at hand. Maintaining momentum requires that site leaders and teachers continuously reinforce school priorities, student success indicators, and collaborative inquiry processes. Prior to the beginning of the 2019–2020 school year, Joni Howard had asked the grade-level leaders if the school improvement process was stable enough to have other teachers step in with the leading of improvement efforts. There was consensus that expanding leadership roles among staff would strengthen school climate and culture to sustain improvement efforts and that maintaining an emphasis on three critical success factors would be essential: creating a strategic focus for equitable student growth, clearly delineating improvement strategies, and shaping improvement efforts through collaborative inquiry.

The Path of Progress for Edison Elementary School

After having served as principal at several school sites in Long Beach, Juan Gutierrez came to Edison Elementary shortly before the onset of the COVID-19 pandemic. He immediately recognized the positive mindsets and collective efficacy that existed among an experienced staff. Because of the remote teaching and virtual collaboration that ensued after his arrival, Juan was not yet able to engage staff in the way he had done with past school sites. So what follows are lessons learned from his previous school sites, which will most certainly play out at Edison Elementary upon return to a normal teaching and learning environment.

The principal sets the vision for school-wide systems and the sustainability of high-impact practices. The intention is to create a positive school climate and culture focused on achieving equitable growth in student learning. This is achieved by being visible, developing trust, and nurturing relationships with staff in a way that empowers teacher leaders to become lead learners. The development of personal and social capital among staff promotes a willingness to push each other toward improving practices and student learning results.

It is important to plan with teachers using data to design school-wide professional learning and create clearly delineated strategies that guide school improvement efforts. The key is to structure collaboration time as teaching–learning cycles that extend over recurring 4- to 6-week periods of time. These improvement cycles are driven by the creation of student learning goals and the subsequent implementation informed by evidence of student learning. Over time, the teaching–learning cycles move toward a lesson study model led by teacher teams.

It takes time, effort, and coaching to help a staff become capable and confident and to understand the possibilities that exist for improving student learning. In this regard, it is essential to identify teacher leaders who can serve as grade-level leaders and members of the instructional leadership team. By developing these lead learners who build the capacity of others, principals can instill within the staff a common belief in their collective ability to maximize the impact of teaching on student learning. Building staff confidence by engaging in robust collaborative inquiry cycles is critical because it builds the capacity of teachers to refine and sustain improvement efforts.

Tips and Tools for Taking Action

Creating clarity of focus is the first step in the ongoing journey of achieving equitable growth in student learning. School sites that have established a strategic focus with clearly delineated improvement strategies guided by short improvement cycles are best positioned to continuously improve practices and student learning results. Creating clarity of focus may seem like a simple task, but it is not the same as defining student learning outcomes, identifying high-yield instructional strategies, or monitoring evidence of student learning. These are superficial improvement strategies that do not engage a school site in the deep work of overcoming the problems of practice at the center of prevailing student equity issues. In fact, schools have become so accustomed to "improvement trifecta" (writing student learning goals, being trained on research-based strategies, and analyzing assessment data) that it almost requires an intervention to correct years of ineffective improvement processes. To right these wrongs, a school district or site should consider the following tips for creating clarity of focus.

Guiding Principles

Many school districts and sites will begin the improvement process by identifying a student learning goal, such as achieving 5 percent growth on the annual, state-wide assessment of English language arts. This in itself does not create clarity because there is uncertainty as to whether this is a measurement of district, school, or classroom growth in student learning. Is the desired academic growth for all students or specific student groups? Does it apply to every teacher or only those who support underserved or underperforming students? If it is annual growth, then how much growth should be achieved by the end of a quarter or trimester? There are too many questions and too much uncertainty.

Guiding principles on the other hand inform the daily actions of leaders and teachers as they engage in the work of improving practices and student learning results. In Long Beach, such guiding principles were noted as ensuring equitable opportunities for every student; providing a safe, welcoming, respectful and rigorous learning environment for every member of the school community; and promoting academic growth for every student. Rather than establishing an arbitrary student learning outcome, guiding principles create agreements for engaging in the work at hand and a moral purpose as to what the work is to accomplish. Goals change over time, whereas guiding principles withstand the test of time.

Student Learning Priorities

We had established based on the work of Richard Elmore that tasks predict performance, the implication being that growth in student learning is predicated upon the rigor and complexity of learning tasks occurring within classrooms on a daily basis. Schools and districts miss the mark when setting annual growth targets for student learning growth, when in fact, the focus should be improving teaching and learning at the student desk. A better approach is to define the key cognitive skills that students have not yet demonstrated as part of daily instruction, which if improved, will result in marked growth in student learning outcomes. These had been delineated as close and analytical reading, precise use of rigorous academic language, structured student collaboration and discourse, evidence-based arguments, and evidence-based writing. Key cognitive skills need to be analyzed through artifacts produced by students in the completion of rigorous and complex learning tasks. The two questions for consideration are: "What key cognitive skills are students not demonstrating as part of the completion of rigorous and complex learning tasks?" and "How can teaching and learning be improved so that all students demonstrate the ability to effectively use these key cognitive skills as part of daily classroom instruction?"

In this manner we are shifting away from establishing an annual growth target to focusing teaching and learning on ensuring all students are capable of using the key cognitive skills most critical for achieving academic growth. This can be achieved only by connecting lag outcomes to lead measures and student success indicators. This plays out as teachers and leaders create clear linkages among annual state assessments, local diagnostic or benchmark assessments, and classroom learning tasks. If we do want to achieve a 5 percent annual growth in English language arts, then evidence of student learning needs to be gleaned from local assessments to pinpoint student needs with even more clarity realized by reviewing student work products from classroom learning tasks. As a result, a school site will establish a student learning priority such as close and analytical reading or evidence-based arguments, which become a focus of daily learning tasks.

Student progress is then monitored by local assessments, and ultimately, learning growth is measured by the annual state assessment.

Short-Term Actionable Plan

Once student learning priorities are established, a school site needs to craft an actionable plan that spans over a 9- to 12-week period of time. This is contrary to the customary process of writing a year-long plan for school improvement. Such annual plans typically are connected to funding allocations, adopted programs, and overarching improvement strategies and, therefore, lack the precision and specificity needed to guide short cycles of teaching and learning that develop precision of pedagogy. The benefit of a short-term action plan is the inherent understanding that at the conclusion of an agreed-upon period of time, such as 9 to 12 weeks, student learning progress and the impact of teaching on student learning will be analyzed to refine action steps moving forward. Chris had referenced that in Long Beach the collaborative inquiry visits were connected to site-based improvement plans, and at the conclusion of each inquiry cycle, schools would pivot to adjust and adapt instructional practices and supports to better meet student learning needs.

Creating a short-term action plan is a simple process that has layers of complexity. A sequence of questions is referenced for engaging school staff in the planning process. These questions are designed to engage the site principal and school leadership team in the creation of a one-page action plan to guide school improvement efforts over a 9- to 12-week period of time. And when completed, the school leadership team should share the plan with all staff to receive feedback, capture insights, and further refine action steps, after which, the plan should serve as a common guide for all teachers and teams to engage in the continuous improvement of teaching and learning over the agreed-upon timeframe. At the conclusion of the inquiry cycle, teams of teachers should be prepared to share student progress, the impact on student learning, and next steps moving forward.

1. What are the school-wide priorities and desired growth for student learning?

2. Which student success indicators will best inform the design of student tasks and learning progressions?

3. Which high-yield pedagogical practices will have the greatest impact on improving learning for all students?

4. How will evidence of learning inform both timely student feedback and adjustments of student learning supports?

5. What structures, processes, and supports are needed to develop collective expertise through agile co-learning and productive collaboration?

6. What timeframes should guide our collective efforts with engaging students in short cycles of instruction and improving upon teaching and learning practices?

Collaborative Inquiry Cycles

Having an actionable plan is not the outcome, rather it is the starting point from which school sites focus the collective efforts of staff as they engage in an agile improvement process. Improvement efforts are driven by recurring collaborative inquiry cycles that consist of four phases: analyze, design, implement, and refine. Analyze evidence of student learning to clearly define the problems of practice that are barriers to student learning growth. Design improvement strategies and identify evidence of learning for monitoring student progress and the impact of teaching on student learning growth. Implement the improvement strategies, and make adjustments along the way based on the evidence of impact on student learning. Refine improvement strategies by analyzing evidence to clarify what works best and why so that improvement efforts can be improved upon moving forward. Repeat the process as part of recurring 3- to 4-week teaching and learning cycles, the goal being that two to three collaborative inquiry cycles can be completed within the timeframe delineated in the school action plan: 9 to 12 weeks. In doing so, teachers and leaders within a school site will gain key insights as to the specific learning needs of students and how to effectively use high-impact instructional practices. As the year unfolds, school sites will gain clarity and develop the capacity to become "laboratories of innovation" in pursuit of equitable growth in student learning.

Taking Action

In working with more than 500 school sites in the process of creating clarity of focus, Jay and the team at InnovateEd have found that two tools are most impactful for guiding school improvement efforts: a collaborative inquiry model (Figure 2.3) and a school action plan template (Figure 2.4). By simply authoring, implementing, and continually updating a short-term action plan using an agreed-upon collaborative inquiry process, school sites over time come to have the clarity of focus and precision of practice needed to achieve the desired growth in student learning. The site principal and teacher leaders of the school leadership team should author the action plan and engage the staff in recurring collaborative inquiry cycles to improve teaching and learning. District leaders should work in collaboration with school sites as co-learners and co-leaders of school improvement efforts. The result will be a sense of empowerment and confidence among school staff in navigating a coherent path to achieve equitable growth in student learning.

Figure 2.3 The Collaborative Inquiry Cycle

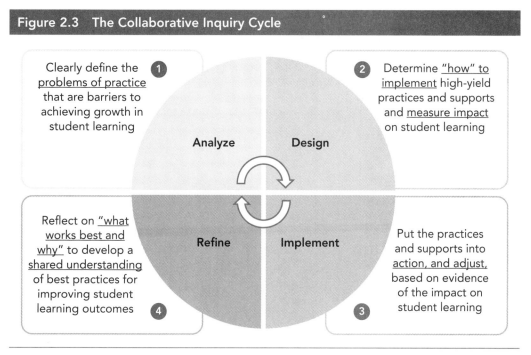

1 Clearly define the <u>problems of practice</u> that are barriers to achieving growth in student learning

2 Determine <u>"how" to implement</u> high-yield practices and supports and <u>measure impact</u> on student learning

4 Reflect on <u>"what works best and why"</u> to develop a <u>shared understanding</u> of best practices for improving student learning outcomes

3 Put the practices and supports into <u>action, and adjust,</u> based on evidence of the impact on student learning

Analyze · Design · Refine · Implement

© 2022 InnovateEd

Figure 2.4 School Action Plan Template

Focus: Which school-wide priorities aligned with district goals will guide the improvement of student learning results?

Outcomes: What measurable outcomes of student progress will define the success of school improvement efforts?

STUDENT SUCCESS INDICATORS	INSTRUCTIONAL SUPPORTS	SCHOOL-WIDE SUPPORT SYSTEMS	EVIDENCE OF LEARNING	IMPLEMENTATION TIMEFRAME
Which academic skills and behaviors are most critical for all students to complete rigorous and complex tasks and to achieve equitable growth in student learning?	Which high-yield strategies and supports will have the greatest impact on developing these critical student skills, and how best can school site practices be implemented to maximize impact?	How will school leaders and teachers collectively engage in job-embedded professional learning that builds capacity to implement high-yield practices informed by the evidence of student learning growth?	How will student learning evidence be monitored and measured to inform timely adjustments of classroom and school-wide support systems for teaching and learning?	What timeframes will guide collaborative inquiry cycles that focus, monitor, and refine school-wide action steps and drive the continuous improvement of staff practices and student learning results?

© 2022 InnovateEd

Cultivating Shared Leadership 3

The purpose of shared leadership is to grow the capacity of a group to co-lead their improvement efforts. This takes shape as a dynamic and interactive influence process among individuals for which the objective is leading one another to achieve agreed-upon goals (Pearce & Conger, 2003). Two underlying factors affect the extent to which shared leadership is cultivated within a school. First is a mutual understanding of leadership as a process that can be taught, shared, distributed, and collaboratively enacted. And the other is collectively recognizing leadership as contextual, in that specific knowledge, skills, and abilities are required based on the demands of the task at hand. The implication is that shared leadership is a social endeavor requiring clarity of focus for the work at hand, a structured process for co-leading improvement efforts, and collective capacity to navigate changes in practice for achieving agreed-upon outcomes.

The paradox of shared leadership is that the ability to positively influence the actions of others is strengthened by empowering individuals within a group to succeed on their own merits. This is in contrast to the perception that leadership is defined by the unique traits, skills, or abilities of an individual whom a team relies on for guidance and support. In fact, the most effective leaders strive to become less relevant so that groups and teams develop a common belief in their collective capacity to overcome challenges, improve practices, and achieve results. A well-known Ted Talk by Derek Sivers (2015) titled "How to Start a Movement" reinforces this concept by illustrating that leaders stand alone in the work at hand until the first followers choose to take action, which in turn serves as the catalyst for moving forward the work of the group. The co-leadership of a few group members exerts the greatest influence on moving the group at large to take action. The role then of a leader is to empower and grow the capacity of the group to co-lead improvement efforts and, in doing so, become less relevant and needed for sustaining the most critical work at hand. To further reinforce this social influence, McKinsey's research has shown that a mere 25% of staff co-leading improvement efforts constitutes the critical mass needed to overturn deeply embedded behaviors and enable transformational changes (Bachmann et al., 2021).

Early in his career Jay served as administrator of leadership development for a county office of education that supported almost 500 schools among 21 school districts, which in total enrolled more than 400,000 students. One of the premier service offerings was a school leadership team training attended by cohorts of principals and key teacher leaders that extended over a 2-year period. Over time, it was discovered that on the first day, professional learning teams could be identified with the highest likelihood of demonstrating the shared leadership needed to move forward the work of improving teaching and learning. This indicator of success was the observable social interactions and influence that existed among school site team members. The contrasts were obvious and could be categorized as follows:

1. The principal was autocratic and teachers were silent, disempowered, and compliant.

2. The principal was amiable, and teachers were cliquish with competing agendas.

3. The principal was disengaged, and teachers were frustrated, anxious, and obstinate.

4. The principal demonstrated silent strength, and teachers were confident and competent.

The premise of projecting the degree to which a team exhibits shared leadership is relative to the climate, culture, capacity, and coherence that exists among team members. Observing the attitudes (climate), behaviors (culture), confidence (capacity), and shared depth of understanding (coherence) within the team provides great insights as to the potential of team performance and productivity. To overcome this variance of shared leadership among school teams, one simple strategy was found to have the greatest impact. This was a highly structured process that engaged the principal as lead learner, promoted co-leading of improvement efforts, and provided an opportunity to practice collaborative inquiry. The team was given a prompt to individually share perceived areas of strength and growth for the school as well as suggest a few next steps to move the school forward. The principal was to function as the notetaker and could ask clarifying questions. In an ordered process, each team member shared their thoughts and built upon each other's insights. At the conclusion of sharing, the principal summarized all input from the team and brought forth next steps clarified during the process. The team at large then reflected on this final sharing and came to consensus on a few possible strategies for moving forward and then briefly shared their insights with other school teams in attendance who could ask questions and offer suggestions. Following the activity, all teams debriefed on the process and conceived strategies to further develop shared leadership within their schools.

So why did this engagement strategy, when used repeatedly as part of training sessions, come to reduce variance and build capacity of teams to demonstrate shared leadership? The answer circles back to Albert Bandura, who named this interesting pattern in human behavior "collective efficacy," which is a group's shared belief in its conjoint capability to organize and execute the courses of action required to produce given levels of attainment (Donohoo et al., 2018). The key phrase here is "shared belief in conjoint ability," meaning there is reciprocal appreciation and recognition for the role of each team member in moving forward the work of the group. The most essential finding inferred from this example is that developing collective efficacy to promote shared leadership will occur only if team members are engaged in a structured process that reinforces the value for and positive impact of co-learning and co-leading. In other words, shared leadership must be modeled, practiced, reinforced, and continuously cultivated to sustain the collective efficacy of teams as they navigate the complexities of school improvement efforts.

> Shared leadership must be modeled, practiced, reinforced, and continuously cultivated to sustain collective efficacy.

Problems of Practice and Promising Practices

W. Edwards Deming, who is recognized as the father of the quality movement, had a compelling statement: "Any time the majority of people behave a particular way the majority of the time, the problem is the system and not the people" (Aguayo, 1990). To clarify, organizational systems encompass the positions, roles, responsibilities, processes, and procedures that support people in carrying out the work at hand (Johnson et al., 2015). These constructs can be broken into the categories of who (position and role), what (responsibilities), and how (processes and procedures). So if we follow Deming's logic, the question is whether there is a structural problem caused by misalignment of positions, roles, and responsibilities or a problem stemming from incoherent or poorly executed processes and procedures. Luckily we have an answer. Structural changes will not result in long-term or significant organizational improvement, but rather a behavior change strategy will yield the greatest impact on improved performance and results (McChesney et al., 2012). The challenge at hand is that top-down structural changes are easy to implement, whereas bottom-up behavior change is difficult and requires a strategy for positively influencing climate, culture, capacity, and coherence. That is why enacting a strategy that changes behavior to achieve sustainable improvement is best realized by cultivating shared leadership.

Unfortunately, the approach most often taken by district and school leaders are structural changes even though the desired outcome is improving how people work together. These leaders are likely well intended; however, the prevailing improvement strategies are too focused on managing structures to organize the system rather than developing people within the system. Structural changes direct attention and efforts on who should do what and when rather than how to learn together and attend to the work better. It is important to identify and understand the root causes of these problems of practice that exist within schools. The best way to do so is by unraveling the distinctions between these problems of practice in contrast to promising practices that cultivate shared leadership. An effective lens for this analysis is studying the climate, culture, capacity, and coherence within teams and groups in their efforts to move the work forward.

At the onset of the 2018 school year, our team at InnovateEd along with Michael Fullan and Mary Jean Gallagher had the pleasure of launching a systems improvement partnership with a large urban school district. As is typical, these districts are divided into regions led by local cabinets who support a large number of school sites. Because these geographically defined district regions have similar structures, studying how the work is mobilized by senior leaders, site principals, and teachers offers a treasure trove for identifying problems of practice and promising practices related to shared leadership. In this partnership, collaborative learning sessions comprised engagements with multiple team structures including senior cabinet members, district leadership teams, district leaders and principals, principal collaboratives, school leadership teams, and teacher teams. Essentially, every level of the system participated in co-leading and co-learning that emphasized shared leadership to move forward improvement strategies. Four key lessons were learned from this systemic improvement partnership, which are described in detail in the following sections to promote understanding of how shared leadership takes shape and affects the work at hand.

Silent Messages

Climate is an intangible way of being that stems from underlying values, beliefs, and attitudes that exist within a group or organization. To understand this aspect of shared leadership, the key is to focus not on what people say but rather how they say it. This is imperative because communication is 93% nonverbal (Mehrabian, 1971); 7% of the impact comes from our words, 38% from our tone, and 55% from our body language. "Reading the room" is necessary because the climate of the group or organization is determined from the manner in which communication and dialog occur among group members. Many leaders and team members have a hard time understanding that it is not what you say but rather how you say it that matters most. Sometimes the best-intended people, in trying to clearly and effectively communicate to others, become too focused on what they want to say instead of considering how people will best hear and receive what is to be said. Body language and tone of voice matter most in this regard, and yet not enough attention is focused on these critical elements of effective communication and teamwork.

The tale of two climates existed among the regions of this large urban school district. This could be felt in how district leaders spoke to principals in messaging and shaping the work at hand. Some were demanding and heavy-handed in approach, whereas others were inviting, empathetic, and inquisitive in nature. And the tone of voice and body language were further enlightening in that those with a top-down mentality expressed themselves with intensity and urgency, thus creating a feeling of anxiety. Whereas the more inviting, sincere, and caring tone of others promoted a sense of empowerment and an opportunity to improve. Although the intention was the same in all district regions, it was how the message was felt and expressed that mattered most. Shared leadership can be developed only when leaders of teams or groups communicate in a way that promotes a feeling of being valued, having autonomy, and giving permission to fail forward. And it is not the words stated but rather how the words are expressed that creates a climate wherein team members are empowered to grow personally and willing to improve professionally.

Congruence

Culture takes shape through the interactions (behaviors and actions) among group members as they attend to the work at hand. In the same vein, a culture of productive teamwork germinates from the congruence of words spoken and actions taken by individuals within groups of an organization. We all know the concept of actions speak louder than words, which has been reframed by Fullan (2018) into one of his sticky phrases: walking the talk. For a positive culture to take root, what is said must be reinforced by what is done. In thinking about your leadership team and your leadership practices, ask yourself, "Is there alignment between what is said and what is done?" This is an essential question because many times hidden meanings and agendas are discovered by observing the congruence or lack thereof between the words and subsequent actions of individuals or teams within an organization. Congruency of words and actions is the foundation for developing trust among group members that over time fosters a culture of shared leadership.

The observation of culture among these aforementioned district regions sheds light on two divergent mental models of shared leadership: compliance versus empowerment. In this and many districts shared leadership is defined as compliance; leaders do as their told and by doing so share the burden of the work. Empowerment leads to a lack of control, which scares most leaders, unfortunately. This is important to consider because leadership creates the culture of a school or district, and many times district leaders and principals are not fully aware of how the culture positively or negatively influences shared leadership. In some regions of the district, the incongruence of words spoken and actions taken was at the center of a compliance-oriented culture. This pattern was observed when vision and direction were established and opportunities for taking action were conveyed only to witness a wait-and-see attitude among school teams. This behavior was a result of groups or teams becoming accustomed to hearing a compelling vision with autonomy for moving forward only to later receive explicit direction on what to do and how to do it. A mixed message of words and actions that translates into "wait until you receive explicit directions as to what you are expected to do" or "don't do anything yet because you'll have to change what you're doing." This is the antithesis of trust and empowerment; it is command and control. Ultimately, this leads to a culture of compliance, that is, passively listening to words spoken while anxiously waiting to conform to the actions taken.

In other regions of the district there was a different approach that was attentive to modeling and reinforcing the culture through the words and actions of leaders. A similar vision with autonomy moving forward was expressed, and yet what followed was a pulse of energy and enthusiasm among groups for clarifying what to do and how to do it. The stark difference came from the emphasis on defined autonomy in that words of empowerment were connected to actions promoting inquiry with accountability. In essence, the words spoken focused direction, whereas the actions taken reinforced autonomy within specific boundaries and an expectation to achieve results. This is the foundation for creating a culture of continuous improvement and the linchpin for developing shared leadership that sustains improvement efforts.

Collaborative Innovation

Capacity is simply the confidence and competence that exists within groups that is enacted when attending to the work at hand. Teams that have high confidence and competence demonstrate what is called collaborative innovation, conjoint work resulting in improved capacity, new competencies, and better outcomes. For example, a simple team-building activity that was used internally at InnovateEd consisted of small teams working together to erect the tallest and strongest tower with little guidance and limited time. The goal was to see which teams engaged in collaborative innovation using an inquiry process of iterative improvement, intentionally improving the confidence, expertise, and capacity of the group to meet the demands of the work at hand. Every team wanted to win, but only those collaboratively innovating made the needed adjustments and improvements to find better ways for successfully completing the task. The key insight is that high-performing teams demonstrate both confidence and competence by adding value to and informing the improvement efforts of the team. A team that lacks confidence and competence will not engage in collaborative innovation to seek out better and more effective ways for engaging in the work at hand.

There was found to be a paradox at play that affected the development of shared leadership among the regions of the large urban district. One would assume that when given the opportunity to collectively define and collaboratively implement improvement strategies, school sites would relish the opportunity to lead their own improvement efforts. This was not consistently the case among all schools or within all regions. The dilemma stemmed from the confidence and competence among teams that were charged with leading the work. In reality, the teams that worked within district regions having a culture of compliance functioned differently than those that worked within a culture of continuous improvement, which is not surprising. What was enlightening was the impact of these cultures on the confidence and competence of team members as well as the willingness or ability to engage in collaborative innovation. Simply stated, the root cause of the paradox was that many site leaders and team members had not been afforded the opportunity to practice and apply the process of collaborative innovation and, as a result, had not developed the confidence and competence to collaboratively find better ways of working together to continuously improve outcomes. Collaborative innovation must be a deep-rooted process among teams if the confidence and competence of team members is to be grown for engaging in productive group work. It's not a switch that can be turned on but rather a process that must be continually practiced and nurtured.

Collective Impact

Coherence is the never-ending process of developing shared depth of understanding about the nature of the work and how it affects student achievement (Fullan & Kirtman, 2019). In contrast, collective impact is contextual to the current work at hand. It is about collectively learning how to improve practices and achieve agreed-upon outcomes. Coherence is the process through which a culture of continuous improvement is created by the staff of a school or district, whereas collective impact is how the expertise among school or district staff is harnessed and leveraged to maximize the impact of improvement efforts. The former is culturally driven, and the latter is practice-oriented.

The ability of a group or team to effectively implement complex strategies with precision and accuracy and consistently achieve desired results is the concept of collective impact in action.

Two games can best illustrate collective impact in action: darts and chess. Throwing darts is about precision (a consistent cluster) and accuracy (at the desired target). Chess is a game of strategy that requires a player to mentally map out moves in advance to circumvent the actions of the opponent. If these games were somehow combined into a team sport, then all players would need deep knowledge of complex strategies and be precise and accurate with employing these strategies to consistently win games. The ability of a group or team to effectively implement complex strategies with precision and accuracy and consistently achieve desired results is the concept of collective impact in action.

The desire of many school districts is to become a coherent system, and this focus was also at top of mind among the district regions being referenced. However, coherence can mean different things for district leaders, site principals, and school staff. And this was the case across these district regions. Most school leaders thought of coherence as a common vision and structure that guides the work at hand (all know where they are going and how to get there). For some it meant the alignment of goals, outcomes, and improvement strategies (all are on the same page). And for a few, coherence was seen as a process of collectively learning how to continuously improve practices and maximize the impact on student learning outcomes (the journey toward realizing collective impact).

The distinctions among these three perceptions become clearer when framed as 1) creating a common vision and direction; 2) aligning goals, outcomes, and strategies; or 3) establishing mutually agreed-upon improvement processes for maximizing the impact on student learning. This third perspective, collective impact, has become known by educators in Long Beach Unified School District (LBUSD) as "The Long Beach Way" and is the most effective strategy for school districts to sustain equitable growth in student learning. The critical insight is that vision, structure, and alignment will never lead to sustainable improvement. The key is engaging teachers and leaders in a way that harnesses and leverages their expertise so that their collective efforts maximize the impact on student learning growth.

District and School Story

A few weeks had passed since the last school visits, and Principal Jacob Westfall continued to contemplate the reasons for the divergence among the schools in his own district. His school leadership team was convening this afternoon, so he considered sharing insights with them to get their feedback. Toward the conclusion of the meeting, Jacob shared a generalized overview of his own learnings from visiting other school sites, and opened up the conversation to gather thoughts from his teacher leaders. Almost immediately the dialog among the teachers focused on the leadership of site principals as well as the comfort and capability of the school staff to work together as productive teams. More senior teachers thought that principals probably

(Continued)

(Continued)

lacked leadership skills, and novice staff questioned whether staff members collaborated effectively. Clearly, Jacob thought, this was a reflection of the dynamics at play within his own school. This was enough information for Jacob, as in his mind the next visit to school sites should focus on principal leadership and teacher collaboration. His next task was to coordinate with his assistant superintendent, Erin McFarland, and fellow principals to frame the purpose of the next visits.

The next week Jacob and Erin were set to meet the four site principals and their teacher leaders for a short after-school meeting at each school site. In preparation, Erin had asked that they use a series of questions to capture relevant and consistent information from each school. The questions were simple and open-ended in the hopes that school staff would be comfortable sharing in the presence of their peers.

1. How would you describe leadership among site administrators and teachers?

2. How comfortable are teachers with leading collaboration and the work of colleagues?

3. What do you think would strengthen shared leadership and collaboration at your school?

Erin was somewhat nervous about the first site visit because she was not sure how teachers would respond to questions with a district administrator in the room. Jacob was more concerned that principals would not be open in their sharing, which would stifle the conversations among teachers. The sequence of visits was to be the same as last time so that information gathered would parallel the blank chart that was in hand and tucked away for in-between visit reflections. This time the charting of information from schools focused on collaborative culture, leadership capacity, impact on school improvement, and questions for consideration.

Both entered the room of the first school, noted as being "compliant," with an open mind and a welcoming presence in an effort to set the stage for a productive dialog. Erin greeted the principal and teacher leaders, and Jacob framed the purpose as a learning opportunity. The site principal set the tone by giving an overview of school priorities aligned with the district vision, goals, and outcomes. And then he expressed his appreciation for how well staff were supporting these improvement efforts. There was a long pause before the first teacher spoke, and rather than sharing insights, the question asked was: "What does the district office want to know about our school?" Erin responded immediately by reinforcing that there was no intention other than learning how school staff collaborated and the ways in which teachers and site administrators engaged in shared leadership. What followed was surprising to both Jacob and Erin. The principal described Wednesday collaboration time, agendas and minutes for these days, and how this kept the staff on track to do the work that was being asked of them. Clearly collaboration was about structure, and leadership was focused on attending to predefined work. For Jacob this felt more like management, and to Erin this seemed to reinforce a compliance mentality of doing the work defined by the district. The last question for the school was to inquire how collaboration and shared leadership could be further strengthened. And again, the dialog went back to improving structures and expectations for staff participation during Wednesday collaboration time. Upon walking to the parking lot, Erin and Jacob both agreed that for this school, shared leadership existed only within the confines of the 45 minutes of weekly collaboration, which was more about completing the task at hand efficiently and effectively—management of a structure.

On the next afternoon, the same process was to be used at the next school, which was initially thought to be "rogue" and later considered to be "prescriptive" due to the prevailing beliefs that the school was doing great work and didn't need to deviate from their plan of action. Both Erin and Jacob wanted to better understand how this deep sense of confidence and competence had manifested among site administrators and teachers. What was learned was both enlightening and frightening in that affirmation and recognition were found to be the primary drivers. As the dialog among the school staff unfolded, it was conveyed that when the school opened, a majority of staff were the best teachers from other schools. The principal had opened the school 5 years ago and handpicked staff from a large pool of exceptional teachers. In fact, the principal shared her appreciation for the staff in looking back at

(Continued)

(Continued)

the past 5 years of success. But most of the conversations circled back to how good the staff were individually and how well students learned in each of their classrooms. When Erin asked how the school came to decide what to do and how to do it collectively, there was a strange silence in the room. One of the most vocal teachers stated, "We are very good at what we do as professionals, and are unique in how we instruct our students." Jacob then inquired how the school knew whether the instructional priorities and practices were benefiting all students in every classroom. And the overwhelming feedback was that the families attending the school were happy with the way teachers were supporting their students. Erin could not help herself and asked a judgmental question, "What evidence do you have that all students are succeeding equally in the school?" This was the end of the conversation based on the body language of staff and the expression of the principal. Jacob and Erin politely thanked the school staff for their time and made their way to the parking lot. Although not voiced by either, the consensus was that neither productive collaboration nor shared leadership was occurring at the school. An adult-centered culture fueled by affirmation and recognition had diminished the desire or perceived need for continuous improvement; good was the enemy of great at this school.

A few days later, Erin asked Jacob to meet a little earlier in advance of the school visit that day. She was remorseful and apologetic for her judgmental tone at the last school site. Jacob stopped her immediately and, to her surprise, thanked her for asking a tough question and shared that these types of questions needed to be asked more often to change the culture of the district. In fact, he thought that principals should be asking this question more often to staff, and the more principals heard this question from district personnel, the more likely it would be asked by principals to their staffs. Erin saw this as a fine line but appreciated the feedback.

Engaging this next school had to be done delicately because both knew this was a "fragmented" school with a challenging staff led by the third principal in 5 years. So the decision was made for the principal to start off and lead the dialog so that Jacob and Erin would be perceived as participants rather than facilitators of the sharing process. Not too far into the meeting, the principal asked the staff to share how they were working together on the school priorities. A first-year teacher seemed eager to speak, and so Jacob prompted her to share. She was genuine in stating that if there were better and more effective ways for improving student literacy and critical thinking skills, then she would gladly learn how to use them. At that moment almost every staff member in the room seemed uncomfortable and shifted a little in their chairs. Erin knew that the right question had been laid on the table and nudged Jacob to follow up. So as not to usurp the leadership of the site principal, Jacob simply inquired, "So how do you as a staff work together and with your principal to figure out better ways of supporting student learning?" Another teacher seemed to be emboldened by the dialog and tactfully stated that the staff didn't do this well, but he very much looked forward to the opportunity to do so with his colleagues. Seizing on the opportunity, the site principal asked, "How can I best support you all to do this together?" What was intended as an information-gathering session had transitioned into what was observed by Erin and Jacob as one of the first times staff had engaged in the conversation of shaping collaboration and forming shared leadership. Erin suggested that she and Jacob could make their exit so that the principal and teachers could continue in this productive dialog. Upon entering their car, Jacob expressed his feeling of hope and excitement for the school as today felt like the beginning of better times to come. Erin agreed and mentioned that she had some ideas as to how the central office could provide structure and support for principals and their staffs to have these rich conversations focused on moving the work forward.

Erin and Jacob were excited to visit the final school because, during their last visit, the school had been found to be "coherent" and had many key aspects in place for leading the continuous improvement of teaching and learning. The room was set up differently, with classroom desks in a circular fashion. Two teachers introduced themselves to Erin and Jacob and shared that they were chosen to be the facilitators of the meeting and had the questions to guide the dialog. There was an ordered sharing process so that every teacher had the opportunity to share their

(Continued)

(Continued)

insights and suggestions for improvement. And the principal thanked all teachers for their input, did a good job connecting all ideas, and then framed what she had witnessed at the school and how she could support many of the ideas shared in moving forward. This all moved rather quickly and allowed Jacob and Erin to ask more informal questions. The first question inquired how teachers and the principal had worked together to plan the flow of the meeting. The response was that it was modeled after how they engage in collaboration and how they work together as a leadership team, which led to another question framed for understanding how teachers were selected to attend this after-school meeting. One teacher spoke up, "We thought you wanted to meet with our leadership team. We're the leadership team, and we represent the school and support the work of our teacher teams." Seeing a smile on Erin and Jacob's faces, another teacher asked whether they wanted to hear more explicit details about their work. And so the rest of the meeting was more of a deep dive into the work of each teacher team and how the teacher leaders in the room were shaping, guiding, and supporting these efforts. After the meeting, Erin appeared to be in a daze, and so Jacob asked what she was thinking. She sternly said, "Why did I not know what this school was doing? Why have I not taken the time to have these conversations with school sites in the past? Why don't schools seem to know what the others are doing and, more importantly, how they're doing it?" Jacob saw the frustration on Erin's face and suggested that they should meet the next afternoon in her office to capture their insights from the visits.

Erin had printed out a large blank chart in advance of the meeting, which was now on the meeting room wall. She asked Jacob if he was open to using sticky notes to capture ideas, stick them onto the poster, and then condense common themes for completing the chart. The process seemed good to Jacob, and so both spent time individually writing notes and filling up the space. They combined concepts and trends to write onto the chart for a final product (Figure 3.1). After about an hour of work, they both sat down and digested the insights they had captured.

Figure 3.1	Key Indicators of School Culture and Capacity			
SCHOOL PROFILE	**COLLABORATIVE CULTURE**	**LEADERSHIP CAPACITY**	**IMPACT ON SCHOOL IMPROVEMENT**	**QUESTIONS TO BE CONSIDERED**
Compliant	Collaboration is seen as a structure that organizes and guides work to be done by teams of teachers.	The primary focus is management of the structures, agendas, and outcomes that define the work.	Staff doesn't have ownership of the work and act as passive participants of predefined tasks.	Why is school staff not taking a more active role in the shaping and leading of their own work?
Prescriptive	Talent, affirmation, and recognition of individuals is seen as more important than collaboration.	Shared leadership is not seen as being essential because the school is recognized for doing well.	Staff do not have a perceived need or agreed-upon process for improving practices or results.	Why is there a lack of desire among staff to use evidence for validation and improvement?
Fragmented	There has not been a structured process for staff to engage in defining how best to work together.	There is a desire among many staff to co-learn and co-lead, but there is not a structure or process.	Staff have not had an opportunity to develop the tools or skills needed for co-leading the work.	Why does the staff resist learning how to work together for improving practices and student results?
Coherent	Staff have agreed-upon processes that guide collaboration and are comfortable facilitating teams.	Staff have capacity to lead and improve both the structures and processes that guide their work.	The school has a collaborative inquiry process that is used by all for continuous improvement.	What has had the most impact with empowering and building capacity of teacher leaders?

© 2022 InnovateEd

(Continued)

(Continued)

Erin thought that it would be beneficial to compare the previous chart of climate and culture to that of collaborative culture and leadership capacity. This led to a few realizations that they agreed to share at the next principals meeting as key learnings from their action research. Erin was cautiously optimistic as to how principals would receive this information and was unsure how best to engage them in this conversation. Jacob was more focused on his own school in wondering how this information could be beneficial for his staff and leadership team.

1. School climate and culture shape the way staff work together, which greatly influences the productivity of collaboration and the development of shared leadership.

2. A shared belief in and common value for collaboration and shared leadership is essential.

3. Structures and processes are critical for productive collaboration and shared leadership but can also be limiting factors if imposed upon versus collectively created.

4. Shared leadership must be nurtured and developed through modeling by principals and ongoing reinforcement from teacher leaders. Deliberate practice builds capacity.

Nurturing a Resilient Climate of Co-Learning

One may wonder why a climate of co-learning needs to be nurtured because it seems intuitive to work with others to become better together. A reason for this need to nurture can be inferred from Bayles and Orland (1993) in *Art & Fear*, which explains "quantity breeds quality" in that 70% of interactions among teams and groups will be mediocre, 20% will be terrible, and 10% will be amazingly productive. Those who want quality co-learning interactions must engage in a large quantity of interactions first to experience and then replicate productive co-learning. In other words, co-learning will never start off productively and requires investing a lot of time working with others to learn how to engage in productive group work. Thus, co-learning must be nurtured because it takes time to learn how to do it well and want to do it more often. It's not a short-term endeavor and needs to be seen as a long-term venture.

But what happens in organizations and teams is that these mediocre and sometimes perceived terrible co-learning experiences cause the quantity of interactions to be diminished or actually halt. And therefore, the quality of interactions never improves, and productive co-learning doesn't evolve. Someone has to be the nurturer, so that over time a climate with an affinity for co-learning emerges within and among school staff. The question is, whose role is it and how best can they attend to doing it? Jay, in working with Dr. Richard DuFour for many years, has captured his insights and experience to provide clarity for this challenge. To paraphrase his thinking, "You can't change people's beliefs, but you can provide an opportunity for people to have new experiences that change their attitudes and, over time through repeated interactions, will change their beliefs." This is Climate Change 101 in action. So focus on how people will interact and work together to provide experiences that over time result in productive co-learning; quantity breeds quality. The school principal in collaboration with key teacher leaders is best positioned to model, facilitate, and reinforce quality interactions and productive co-learning. Michael Fullan has a similar change theory that lays it out with utter simplicity: "Name it, model it, and monitor it." In this case, "monitor" can be replaced by "nurture."

In moving from the key insights of Rick DuFour and Michael Fullan to more pragmatic examples in action, one can look toward the work that Chris led in Long Beach. As had been already noted, a 9- to 12-week collaborative inquiry visit (CIV) had been established that engaged school sites with central office staff in the process of co-leading improvement efforts. Schools would design action plans with clearly delineated strategies for achieving growth in student learning for these multiple-week periods of time and then monitor progress, assess impact, and refine action steps moving forward. The naming of the CIV was essential because this brought forth a common meaning to the concept of a collaborative inquiry cycle that by design, empowered school sites to guide their own improvement efforts with central office staff support. This process however was not in name alone; it was highly structured with district leaders and site principals co-modeling the agile improvement process until all school sites had a deep level of comfort with the agreed-upon practices. Over the 18 years that Chris served as superintendent, and continuing after his departure, these recurring cycles of CIVs continued to be reinforced every 9 to 12 weeks with each school site. One could sum this up as "redundancy builds fluency" and that through consistency and ongoing reinforcement, translates into a shared understanding of the way we do things here, that is, "The Long Beach Way."

Cultivating Collaborative Inquiry

At this point in the book, there have been many references to the meaning of as well as the structures and processes for engaging in collaborative inquiry. Unfortunately, this term has become somewhat of a cliché because it is used fairly loosely by educators at a surface level to describe what they do. Collaborative inquiry is most often a label used synonymously with teacher collaboration. So it is important to more closely compare traditional collaboration to the explicit nuances of engaging in collaborative inquiry. In doing so, we will clarify the meaning of and identify the actions that cultivate a culture of collaborative inquiry.

For the past 20 years collaboration in schools has been promoted through the professional learning community (PLC) movement. The initial focus was creating time to collaborate, which prompted educators to adapt and adjust work schedules to afford job-embedded collaboration during the school day. And once this protected time was in place, the effective use of collaboration time became the emphasis. The four questions of a PLC authored by DuFour and Eaker (1998) was most widely used as a loose framework:

1. What do we want all students to know and be able to do?

2. How will we know if they learned it?

3. How will we respond when some students do not learn?

4. How will we extend the learning for students who are already proficient?

This led to three primary objectives for the effective use of collaboration time: identifying essential standards, designing formative assessments, and analyzing evidence to target student support. To formalize the PLC process, many schools developed agendas, protocols, and minutes documenting their work that was defined by topics such as "what is to be taught," "what is the assessment," and "what tiered supports should students receive based on evidence of learning." Most often, though, what did not happen was a change in teaching practices or adjustments to the student learning process. In many schools, collaboration devolved into a teaching and assessing cycle. This was never the intent of the PLC movement or that of Richard DuFour, the forefather of this important work.

Collaborative inquiry may be more easily understood through the construct of the lesson study model. In fact, the school that was originally led by DuFour as both principal and superintendent evolved from a more traditional PLC to a lesson study approach. Collaborative inquiry always starts with reviewing evidence to understand the problems of practice among students that are barriers or constraints to higher levels of learning. This process leads to the formulation of an essential question and theory of action. For example, if a school identified that students did not have the critical thinking skills necessary for interpreting information and using evidence to explain or justify reasoning, then the essential question could be framed as "How can we develop students to become more capable with interpreting information and using evidence to explain or justify reasoning?" A theory of action would then frame how teachers test an approach for improving teaching and learning. This could be stated as "If students use structured notetaking for capturing evidence and have sentence frames for using evidence to support explanations and justifications, then students will be able to speak and write in a way that more clearly communicates their thinking." After that would be a discussion of how teaching and learning would occur followed by teachers implementing strategies and adjusting instruction based on the observable impact on student skill development. Last, student work samples and observations of student learning would be used as a means of more deeply understanding the teaching and learning process for both reflection and refinements moving forward. Collectively, this could be framed as analyzing evidence to define the problems of practice, designing a theory of action and methods of teaching to support student learning, implementing and adjusting instruction based on student learning impact, and refining teaching and learning practices through the analysis of evidence. The key is that the problems of practice and theory action have to be of significant importance for accelerating the learning of all students.

Collaboration is a structure for working together to improve student learning results, whereas collaborative inquiry is a mindset and process for co-learning and co-leading the improvement of practices to accelerate student learning. Collaboration and collaborative inquiry are not mutually exclusive and should become tightly coupled and ultimately conjoined. Collaboration then becomes not a scheduled activity but rather is understood to be a collaborative inquiry cycle that extends across a set period of time (i.e., 3 to 9 weeks). And this inquiry process is not only for teachers but becomes the strategy for site administrators and district leaders to engage in the work within their own teams and in collaboration with teachers. This is the foundation of shared leadership and systemic collaboration.

Cultivating collaborative inquiry is essential because the initial stages of any improvement effort begin with structural changes, as in the reference to the collaboration structures of a PLC. The goal is to promote cultural change so that collaboration structures result in robust collaborative inquiry processes that maximize the impact of teaching on student learning. Distinguishing as to whether collaboration and inquiry have transitioned from the initial structural change to more impactful cultural change can simply be assessed by seeking to understand the work from the perspective of school site teachers and leaders. Those focused on structural change will note the days, times, and frequency of collaboration; reference the tools and resources that guide collaboration; and share the goals and outcomes that are to be attained through collaboration. In contrast, those engaging in cultural change will communicate the purpose and processes that guide collaboration, emphasize the supports in place for individuals and teams to effectively collaborate, and discuss the desired improvement of practices that are intended to achieve gains in student learning. The first emphasizes what to do, how to do it, and when it is done, whereas the latter focuses on the why and agreed-upon processes and practices for building capacity to sustain improvement efforts: the distinguishing characteristic between structural and cultural change. Cultivating collaborative inquiry can be considered a process through which leaders build the capacity of individuals and teams to co-lead the continuous improvement of practices and student learning results. It starts with the structures for collaboration, then shifts to the processes and practices that guide collaborative inquiry, and results in a collective commitment to sustain improvement efforts through robust collaborative inquiry processes.

Navigating Changes in Practice to Improve Student Learning

Let's assume that a school has a climate of co-learning and a well-established culture of collaborative inquiry for the co-leading of improvement efforts. One would say that the school has cultivated shared leadership. And although there is an appreciation for these structures and processes, there still remains resistance to changing practices for the betterment of student learning. Then what happens? This scenario plays out often and, at times, causes frustration and dismay among school staff and leaders alike. To understand how to navigate changes in practice for improved student learning, we need to return to Albert Bandura's concept of vicarious learning experiences.

It is human nature to want to see change happen and yet be disgruntled when people do not adopt or adapt practices that are proven to achieve better results. However, we can't say, "Do it this way because it's a better way," and expect people to automatically change.

The story of vicarious learning experiences plays out in this fashion. An advertisement was put in the newspaper offering to pay money to people who were willing to be treated for their fear of snakes. About a dozen individuals came to Bandura's office, and he progressed in engaging them in the following treatment activity. First he told them that there was a snake in a cage on the other side of the office door. All were dismayed but eventually followed his lead in peeking through the window on the door to see the caged snake. The next phase was for him to slowly open the door, and each individual would take one step inside the room where the snake was caged. Eventually all took the leap of faith and passed through the doorway. Bandura then shared with all that he was going to walk toward the cage and wanted them to watch his movements and follow his steps when they were ready. Again, all slowly maneuvered to closer proximity of the caged snake. After that, Bandura placed his hand on the cage so that all could see it was safe and asked all to do the same when they felt comfortable. Eventually all took this step as well. Last, Bandura opened the cage and held the snake, allowing all to see its actions and how it was not harmful to him. He asked each person to touch the snake as he held it as a final step in ridding themselves of a lifelong fear. And again, all did eventually. So how long would one think this experimental treatment took Albert Bandura? The answer is surprising. The total time was about 3 hours. And thus, the concept of vicarious learning experiences was conceived. Change can be accelerated when individuals have the opportunity to first observe others engaging in the practice and then use this knowledge to employ the practice themselves. Navigating changes in practice requires a process that supports others through vicarious learning experiences that must be modeled by leaders who are willing and able to do so first.

The key insight here is to not expect people to change practices but instead focus on observing and learning from those already doing the practice to create vicarious learning experiences for those who are more reluctant or resistant to changing practices. But where does energy most often go: toward those who are doing the practice or those who are reluctant or resistant? Listen to the conversations of principals and teachers in a school, and you will not hear an appreciation for those doing the practice. Instead you will hear frustration toward those not doing the practice. And this often is phrased this way: "We need more staff buy-in," "He needs to get on the same page with us," or "She will never be willing to do this." These words, spoken often, have little or no impact on improving practices or student learning. What is needed are more lead learners like Albert Bandura, those who through their actions create vicarious learning experiences that empower and develop confidence among others so they too can experience the same level of success.

Lead learners engage others in navigating the complexities of changing practices by shaping climate and culture (modeling beliefs and behaviors), engaging in collaborative inquiry (a structured process for co-learning and co-leading), and focusing efforts on achieving better results (agreed-upon outcomes). They model specific beliefs and behaviors to support others in co-learning and co-leading for the purpose of achieving agreed-upon outcomes. If you want to accelerate change, then develop more lead learners because this is the ultimate purpose of cultivating shared leadership. But who are the lead learners in a school? The principal and the members of the school leadership team should proactively take on this role of shaping climate and culture and building collective capacity to co-lead collaborative inquiry focused on the improvement of practices and results. This is essential for developing shared leadership and navigating the change process.

> If you want to accelerate change, develop more lead learners.

Denoting school leadership teams and site administrators as change agents is more than a simple identification of a critical team structure. Change is best described by Everett Rogers (1962) through the *diffusion of innovation theory* that describes how more innovative and impactful practices spread across an organization. This has been used with every school and district supported by InnovateEd over the past 15 years and has assisted with dramatically speeding up the change process. The theory states that within any organization, individuals and members of teams fall into the following five categories: Innovators are the 3% of people who openly embrace and are excited to participate in implementing new and innovative practices. Early adopters, 13%, are wise consumers of innovative ideas who take the time to understand first and then quickly try new practices. The early majority, 34%, are more eager to observe others engaging in the more innovative practices and over time will do so themselves when comfortable. The late majority, 34%, are less likely to be aware of changes in practice until these new ways are overtly apparent in the organization. And laggards, the last 16%, are resistant and reluctant to consider changing practices from either the fear of failure or the comfort of the status quo.

Which of these five groups receives the majority of attention when schools are focused on improving or changing practices? Most of the time it is the laggards because we naturally desire buy-in and want to overcome their resistance. However, the focus should be on the innovators and early adopters who are the lead learners and whose actions will accelerate change via vicarious learning experiences. And once the early majority engages, 50% of the staff is invested in changing practices, which will naturally move the late majority as cultural change (behaviors and actions) becomes overt. The laggards will be last, but 80% of staff implementing more innovative practices will have a significant impact on improving student learning. The lesson to be understood here is that the principal and school leadership team must be the innovators and early adopters for change to happen at a productive pace within schools. This is imperative for effectively navigating changes in practice to improve student learning.

The Path of Progress for Northridge Middle School

Richard Ramos has been a principal for 7 years at two school sites in the Los Angeles Unified School District, where he currently serves as principal of Northridge Middle School. Richard was accustomed to top-down directives and expectations for leading school sites and came to Northridge with a mindset that he now refers to as a "cookie-cutter approach," wherein principals drive school change through financial decisions and managing of the instructional program. Although the purpose was to change the school to better serve students, the staff at Northridge were resistant to dismantling established programs in ways that Richard thought would meet the learning needs of all students. Richard knew there needed to be a different approach that promoted shared leadership among staff to guide school improvement efforts.

In year two of his tenure at Northridge, the school began the process of becoming a school on the move by focusing on developing shared leadership. This process was difficult for Richard because he wanted to accelerate change and push improvement efforts rather than develop the capacity of staff to co-lead the improvement of practices and student learning results. Initially, the staff went through a process of establishing shared values and a common vision for what to do and how to do it. This included working with a school leadership team to create ownership among staff of a commonly agreed-upon plan that guided school improvement efforts. At first, the school leadership team consisted of the principal and six teacher leaders. As momentum grew, other staff members wanted to become part of the work because the school leadership team members were actively sharing their progress and impact via an inquiry process that engaged others in attending to the work at hand. Richard recounts that one teacher who had been at the school for 18 years stated that this was the most he had ever talked to and worked with other staff members.

As the staff began engaging in learning walks to develop a common understanding of student needs, a comment was made that students did not seem to be talking at all in classrooms. Most staff came to recognize the lack of collaborative conversations among students as a common problem of practice. This insight fueled a desire among staff to more frequently engage in learning walks and continue in the process of identifying problems of practice and discovering promising practices. By the end of the school year, because of this common focus and desire among staff for improving teaching and learning, there was a marked difference in the academic discourse among students. Principals from other school sites began visiting the school and had their teachers observe classrooms to inform their own practices.

In year three, more staff joined the work of the school leadership team. By this point in time, student learning issues were jointly discussed among staff to identify priorities for improving teaching and learning. Staff began to take ownership of collaborative inquiry processes to guide short cycles of teaching and learning. These efforts improved teacher collaboration and developed commonly agreed-upon practices for improving student learning results. Underperforming students and underserved student groups began to demonstrate more confidence with engaging in collaborative conversations within classrooms. There was a visible effort within all classrooms to implement high-impact practices for improving student collaboration and discourse.

By the end of year three, the professional learning in the school was led by teacher leaders and supported by site administration. This was a significant shift in culture over a short period of time from a desire for autonomy among staff to that of collaborative learning and co-leading of school improvement efforts. The shared leadership proved to be sustainable as the pandemic disrupted education in that staff were capable of co-planning instructional cycles and collectively identifying and overcoming problems of practice. Central to these improvement efforts was an agreed-upon collaborative inquiry process that guided the work of teachers as they pursued better ways of supporting student learning.

Key insights shared by Principal Ramos were that a continuous improvement process driven by a cycle of inquiry is the foundation of shared leadership that promotes collegial collaboration and collective accountability. Developing deep levels of ownership of the work among staff ensures that improvement efforts are sustainable. Shared leadership and collective expertise emerge as staff uncover the barriers to student learning, examine the impact of instructional practices on student academic growth and well-being, and work together to overcome challenges and improve practices.

The Path of Progress for Kolb Middle School

In 2018 InnovateEd began a partnership with Rialto USD to support the improvement efforts of the five middle schools. The reason being that from 2015 to 2018 the growth in district-wide ELA and math proficiency had each increased six percentage points with the former being 50% and the latter 40%. By 2018 the middle school proficiency rates had risen to only 27% in ELA and 14% in math. Clearly there was a need to assist these school sites with improving teaching and learning. At the beginning of the 2018–2019 school year, there was a transition of principals among all middle schools so that improvement efforts for overcoming student learning barriers could be initiated by leaders with fresh eyes. This transition was timely because the superintendent had spent the past 3 years building organizational culture and improving district systems so that school principals could have the support needed to lead site improvement efforts.

Armando Urteaga became principal in the 2018–2019 school year at Kolb Middle School and was formerly the principal of Jehue Middle School for the 7 years prior. At the time of his arrival at Kolb, the school site had been designated as one of the lowest-performing schools in the state, which required an intense focus on achieving growth in student learning. The school was successful with exiting this low-performing status, and what follows is how the school staff attended to these improvement efforts.

The model of support for middle schools was to assist all five school principals by convening multiple times throughout the year to define priorities, overcome problems of practice, and identify high-impact strategies for improving school culture and practices. Each site also participated in school leadership team sessions designed to create short-term action plans that guided school improvement efforts, which were paired with sessions for data analysis, review of student work, and learning rounds to inform teaching and learning practices. The intent was to engage middle schools in an improvement cycle by supporting principals and their school leadership teams to implement robust collaborative inquiry processes for achieving growth in student learning.

Armando discovered that the staff at Kolb were not unified in direction or in the use of agreed-upon processes or practices. Discipline and attendance issues were apparent, which had resulted in the underperformance of student groups and was a root cause for the low-performing school status. The first step was to ensure that all students were in class and actively engaged in daily classroom learning. This emphasis on school climate and culture led to significant growth in the number of students achieving honor roll for the first quarter of the school year. This led staff to become willing to do what Armando phrased as "trust the process." By empowering the staff to take ownership of the improvement process and make decisions as to the changes needed in teaching and learning, this initial positive change in student performance was the catalyst needed to move forward.

Another key aspect was engaging in learning rounds as part of the improvement process. As staff began to more clearly see teaching and learning in action, there was clarity as to what works well in the school to improve student learning. This led to a way for all staff to develop a deeper understanding of the current state of teaching and learning and to identify what could be the focus of improvement efforts moving forward. This allowed the school leadership team to refine the school action plan to zero in on the instructional practices that had the most potential for achieving the desired growth in student learning. Staff were able to maximize the use of weekly collaboration time as well as common prep periods for focused instructional planning and observing other teachers' classrooms.

As a result of developing a school climate and culture with staff ownership of improvement efforts, implementing an action plan focused on high-impact instructional practices, and having support from administrators and the school leadership team to more effectively use collaboration time, Kolb successfully exited from the lowest-performing school designation. Unfortunately, the pandemic occurred the following year, and as a result, state testing was postponed. The staff of Kolb Middle School was not able to know if equal gains in student achievement were realized in subsequent years. Maintaining the school focus on improving practices to achieve growth in student learning remains a priority for the school staff.

The Path of Progress for
Jefferson Leadership Academy

Connie Magee has been principal of Jefferson Leadership Academy, a middle school in LBUSD, for 4 years. She clearly remembers that upon arrival at the school, there was no clear plan that guided improvement efforts, and staff had not been empowered to lead the work. Therefore, the first priority would be to cultivate shared leadership. This process began with revamping individual and team goals to increase ownership among the staff. All teachers used the same goals format, and all teacher, department, and school goals were stored in a shared drive to increase accountability and transparency. The result was shifting from a compliance activity with generic goals to staff ownership of personal goals and action plans for ensuring student success.

Connie also established what she calls the "state of the school." Department teams reflected on goals and data each quarter and shared next steps to the whole staff. Through this process she gathered data from all teachers and departments on campus. Next, she met with the instructional leadership team to determine next steps based on shared consensus, and together they determined the next steps for professional learning. This process led to an agreement among staff as to the instructional strategies and student learning priorities for the school year, and by repeating this process at the end of each quarter, the staff could fine-tune their actions to address current results. Staff began to observe each other and co-learn how to use these strategies effectively. Cross-departmental sharing promoted the development of deeper expertise with agreed-upon instructional strategies. The combination of data-driven goals and common instructional strategies was an effective process for staff to work together collaboratively on a few school-wide priorities.

The next step for Connie was to "groom and grow" the instructional leadership team. The desire was to have this team in collaboration with their colleagues focus the direction of the school and design the support systems needed for improving teaching and learning. Over time, the success among staff with improving teaching and learning led to common agreements and the sustainability of school-wide practices and processes. Connie recognized the need to cultivate a culture of trust by promoting vulnerability and risk-taking among staff, which requires a principal to trust and interact with staff, rather than control the work of staff, and serve as a lead learner. This cultural change was accelerated when Connie took medical leave at the time when the school was relocated to a temporary facility. The staff continued to work together in moving forward the work in her absence. The emerging culture of shared leadership was further strengthened as staff developed confidence and expertise in the co-leading of school improvement efforts.

As the school returned to their campus, Connie took the opportunity to fine-tune collaboration structures such as augmenting the master schedule and ensuring that the rooms of content area teachers were in close proximity. She continued the collaboration processes by working with the instructional leadership team to create department goals connected to goals of individual teachers, which all tied into summative assessment data. Connie has all teachers give the summative assessment each year so everyone has "skin in the game."

In reflecting on the past 4 years at Jefferson Leadership Academy, Connie shared that relationships matter most. Empowering and building the capacity of staff to lead school improvement efforts is equally important as is maintaining a clear school focus with departmental and individual goals for achieving growth in student learning. As a principal, the priority is to co-learn with staff by engaging in the work with them and modeling what it looks like to serve as a lead learner.

Tips and Tools for Taking Action

Cultivating shared leadership is essential if schools are to transform climate, shape culture, and build capacity for the purpose of attending to the critical work of student equity. To do so successfully requires that site principals and teacher leaders nurture a resilient climate of co-learning, cultivate an appreciation for collaborative inquiry, and most importantly, guide staff in navigating changes in practice to improve student learning. None of these actions are simple because they are neither task-oriented nor achieved by structural changes. Cultivating shared leadership calls upon principals and teachers to serve as lead learners who model and reinforce the practices that are desired to be undertaken by school staff. Lead learners are savvy change agents who understand the value of co-learning and the power of co-leading improvement efforts. The following key insights are offered to those who desire to cultivate shared leadership within their school sites and district.

Modeling Co-Learning

In this chapter there have been several references to Jay's work with Richard DuFour, and one story is best suited to frame the concept of modeling co-learning. When Rick had initially become principal of his school site, he was eager to promote co-learning among the staff. Having secured funding from the site parent–teacher association, Rick was excited to share with his staff that funds were available for release time so that teachers could collaborate or observe each other's classrooms. However, by the end of the school year, Rick was dismayed that not one staff member had accessed the funds to engage in co-learning with colleagues. Jay, having heard the story from Rick, was not surprised to find that at the school where he became principal, there was not effective use of collaboration time. His first step was for himself, the assistant principal, counselors, and instructional coach to serve as process observers of teacher collaboration. Each attended collaboration and documented the interactions among staff during collaboration time. These notes were shared with the teams as a way of reflecting on current practices and considering the improvement of practices. Having this information in hand, collaboration was shifted into a whole group model located within the school library. Teachers were seated as teams but were supported as a whole group in learning how to effectively engage in co-learning. As teams observed, listened to, and gleaned key insights from their colleagues, a climate of co-learning emerged among the staff. What was initially a wrote activity without clarity, guidance, or clear outcomes, over time became a time for sharing best practices, discussing student learning needs, and considering how to overcome common problems of practice. Toward the end of the school year, teacher teams returned to collaborating within separate rooms because there had been established a value for and appreciation of co-learning.

Why does co-learning not occur more naturally within schools as opportunities to collaborate arise? As has been discussed in this chapter, initial co-learning interactions tend not to be positive or productive. It takes time to learn how best to work together, develop the norms of collaboration, and build trust within teams. Most often there are a few teams who seem to naturally collaborate well and enjoy productive co-learning. By observing these teams in action, others can gain insights that move their own teams forward. These interactions within teams need to be fostered, nurtured, and supported in a way that brings forth positive outcomes benefiting the work of each individual. There must be opportunities to establish common belief systems and an appreciation for the strengths and needs of each team member. The fastest way to establish a resilient climate of co-learning is to have the school staff work together on overcoming common problems of practices and collectively identifying possible solutions moving forward. And this cannot occur as an isolated activity or be seen as an opportunity but rather has to be structured in a way that staff experience repeated positive interactions and productive outcomes with their peers.

Reinforcing Collaborative Inquiry

Co-learning is a facet of school climate in that it is defined by the extent to which staff value working with and learning from their peers. The natural tendency in schools is to work in isolation within the comfort of individual classrooms. So the first step in cultivating shared leadership is to establish a climate of co-learning wherein working together is valued more than autonomy and isolation. The next step is to reinforce collaborative inquiry as a mindset and structured process for co-leading improvement efforts. When we say mindset it is to distinguish between the concepts of collaborating on a Wednesday afternoon versus the purpose and outcomes of working together. The first is an activity denoted by a date and time, and the latter is a collective understanding of productive group work and how to achieve agreed-upon outcomes. All too often teachers show up to collaboration time either expecting an agenda to guide their work or wanting autonomy to have unstructured dialog around urgent tasks and demands. This is where a structured process is essential for collaborative inquiry. In this chapter we have noted that a collaborative inquiry process has four phases: analyze, design, implement, and refine. Analyze evidence of student learning to define the problems of practice that are barriers to student learning growth. Design improvement strategies and identify evidence to monitor the impact of agreed-upon strategies on student learning. Implement the strategies and adjust along the way based on the impact on student learning. Refine improvement strategies by analyzing evidence to clarify what works best and why so that strategies are improved upon moving forward. When teachers and leaders have a common mindset and an agreed-upon process for co-leading improvement efforts, collaborative inquiry becomes the most powerful strategy for achieving equitable growth in student learning.

The way that Jay and the team at InnovateEd have supported school sites to reinforce collaborative inquiry is by linking four sequential collaboration times to form an inquiry cycle. This is simply accomplished by connecting four Wednesdays to create a 4-week collaborative inquiry cycle then establishing that the purpose of the first Wednesday is to engage in the phases of analyzing evidence to establish learning priorities and designing improvement strategies with some form of evidence for monitoring student progress. The second and third Wednesdays focus on implementing, adjusting, and improving teaching and learning both individually and in collaboration with team members. The fourth Wednesday is dedicated to analyzing data and student work or, at times, conducting learning rounds as a means to develop common understanding of what has worked best in supporting student learning and why so that all team members have clarity of action for the next cycle of inquiry. Chris in his work at Long Beach used a CIV at 9- to 12-week intervals that served as both the end point and beginning of recurring inquiry cycles. The purpose was to assess progress and impact, identify what works best and why, and agree upon which strategies will best support student learning moving forward. What is most important is that collaborative inquiry is structured as recurring cycles that guide school site teachers and leaders in the co-leading of improvement efforts within their own school site. And over time the recurring inquiry cycles strengthen the shared leadership within the school to overcome the prevailing barriers preventing students from achieving growth in learning.

Navigating Changes in Practice

So if a school staff has embraced a climate of co-learning and developed an appreciation for collaborative inquiry, then one would assume that as a result there will be improvement in practices and student learning results. Unfortunately this is not always the case because a collaborative staff does not necessarily change practices for the betterment of student learning. It is not that the staff is against change, rather it is what Pfeffer and Sutton (2000) have coined as the "knowing–doing gap." Fear is the primary reason that staff are resistant to taking action in spite of a clear understanding as to how practices can be improved. For some it is comfortability with current practices, for others it is not wanting to fail, and for the rest it is uncertainty as to whether a new approach will achieve better results. Regardless, it comes down to fear of change, failure, or the unknown. To overcome this resistance we have referenced the work of Albert Bandura and the concept of vicarious learning experiences. An effective change strategy always employs lead learners who are willing and able to demonstrate for others what the improved practice looks like in action. By modeling, reinforcing, and providing opportunities for others to engage in a new practice through easy and incremental steps, a school staff develops the confidence and competence needed to navigate the change process.

Who are these lead learners, and how do we find more of them? The reality is that the school principal needs to be the lead learner whose top job is grooming teacher leaders to also serve in this capacity. This small group of lead learners is more formally known as the school leadership team. As has been noted, research by McKinsey has brought to light that only 25% of staff co-leading improvement efforts will overturn deeply embedded behaviors and enable transformational changes. So the third step in cultivating shared leadership is to develop a school leadership team who is capable of navigating the changes in school site practices. Change is a plus one process, meaning that to enact change, those leading the work simply engage one other person in the work at hand, which equates to 50% of the staff. Another plus one is 75%, and the last group equates 100%. That's only three levels of staff engagement to move an entire school forward in the change process. Often, though, the change process is approached as a complex endeavor rather than dividing staff into four groups and engaging in three levels of co-learning and collaborative inquiry. In this manner change becomes a strategy and not an outcome. We don't change people, rather we use a change strategy to develop the capacity and confidence of people to change themselves.

Taking Action

To come full circle on cultivating shared leadership, employing a change strategy is taken on by the principal and members of the school leadership team as they create a climate of co-learning and engage in collaborative inquiry for the purpose of navigating changes in school practices to improve student learning results. These lead learners serve as change agents by developing the confidence and capacity of staff members to co-learn and co-lead school improvement efforts. Because shared leadership can be an intangible concept, it is important to name, model, and reinforce school improvement processes and practices in a visual manner. One tool has proven to be most effective: a planning template for creating an agreed-upon collaborative inquiry cycle (Figure 3.2). This tool is effective because it requires members of a school team, the school staff, or a group of principals or district leaders to come to consensus as to how they will delineate the action steps of the inquiry process. Doing so promotes a climate of co-learning because the process reinforces productive collaboration and completion of a common task. Then team members must enact the inquiry process as part of a 4- to 6-week learning cycle that fosters a culture of collaborative inquiry through recurring cycles of co-learning and co-leading. And as problems of practice are addressed by agreed-upon improvement strategies, individuals become more comfortable and confident with navigating the change process.

Figure 3.2   Collaborative Inquiry Cycle Planning Template

Clearly Define the problem(s) of practice

Our problem(s) of practice is . . .

Evidence and insights that informed this decision are . . .

This focus area is a barrier/constraint to learning because . . .

Design Strategies Informed by Evidence

Our strategies moving forward are . . .

If done successfully, then we expect that . . .

Evidence that best informs our actions will be . . .

Analyze | Design

Refine | Implement

What Works Best and Why?

We will analyze impact and share insights by . . .

To deepen our understanding, we will be explicit, precise, and concise by focusing on . . .

Our norms that promote transparency and vulnerability for improving practices will be . . .

Take Action and Adjust

We will implement our strategies by . . .

The period of time for implementation will be . . .

As we implement, adjustments will focus on . . .

© 2022 InnovateEd

Developing Collective Expertise 4

Many extended conversations occurred around the topic of developing collective expertise as the writing of this book unfolded. During one conversation, Jay had brought up the perception from outsiders that there was a mystique about Long Beach Unified School District (LBUSD) in respect to the deep capacity for high-quality teaching and learning. This conversation had a significant impact on Chris as he reflected on the years of work within Long Beach. He was surprised by the comment and clearly had been considering why others had this sense of wonder as to how Long Beach had developed such deep and collective expertise. His statement was insightful, "There is no mystique in Long Beach. It's about having an intentional and consistent focus on student equity. Long Beach administrators and teachers are equity warriors."

This is the key ingredient for developing collective expertise: having a shared purpose that drives and sustains equitable growth in student learning. It is not expertise in effectively using specific instructional strategies, formatively assessing student learning, or engaging in collaborative inquiry. The mystique comes not from the practices but rather the purpose of the practices: student equity. How many times have we heard school sites or central offices give praise about the effective use of instructional practices or student engagement strategies and, similarly, celebrate gains in student achievement results? These recognitions tend to be a way of promoting better use of strategies and realizing more gains in student achievement. It's kind of a bumper sticker mantra; teach better and learn more. But this approach does not have the power of what Chris noted of intentionally and consistently being equity champions.

Simon Sinek (2011) may have expressed this best in his description of the golden circle, which illustrated how high-performing organizations start with the why (purpose), then reinforce the how (process), and finally mention the what (practices and outcomes). Chris and LBUSD attended to the work in a way that most others do not—focusing improvement efforts on a shared purpose, co-creating processes for attending to the work, and empowering schools to learn how to develop collective expertise for achieving agreed-upon outcomes—whereas others focus on the degree to which practices were implemented with fidelity and similar results are attained by all. Chris and his team at Long Beach have played the long game of sustainability, whereas many other districts and school sites continue to play the short game of quick wins. Developing collective expertise takes the discipline of a marathon runner rather than the short-lived endurance of a sprinter.

So how can collective expertise be developed for the purpose of reducing equity gaps and accelerating the learning of all students? It begins with clearly and redundantly reinforcing a shared purpose of student equity then plays out as a robust collaborative inquiry process that by design and over time creates instructional coherence and precision of pedagogy. And when pulling back the layers, one will find four factors are at the core of developing collective expertise: student equity, instructional coherence, collaborative inquiry, and precision of pedagogy.

Problems of Practice and Promising Practices

Developing collective expertise to continuously improve teaching and student learning does not have to be a complex endeavor, but it does have to be the purpose of district and school improvement efforts. As noted, it's not about an initiative focused on a specific instructional model, implementing an improvement science framework, or raising test scores for certain student groups. These are certainly viable tools and worthy outcomes, but each creates complexity and can unintentionally result in superficiality. A famous phrase from Grady Booch captures the essence, "a fool with a tool is still a fool," which implies that one must directly address the issues that stand in the way of improving instructional capacity and realizing gains in student performance. Tools don't build capacity for achieving better results because growth in student learning is predicated upon the improvement of practices. A better phrase for consideration is "improvement of practices precedes growth in student learning." And this cannot be a solitary affair but rather a collective effort if equitable growth in

Four factors are at the core of developing collective expertise: student equity, instructional coherence, collaborative inquiry, and precision of pedagogy.

learning is the ultimate outcome. Developing collective expertise is simply an agreed-upon process that engages all staff within a school in the relentless pursuit of learning how best to meet the learning needs of all students in their care. The key question is, "What is your agreed-upon process for developing collective expertise?"

In comparing our experiences over the past 18 years in education, Chris as superintendent of LBUSD and Jay as a consultant supporting the improvement efforts of superintendents, there are many similarities in how we have attended to capacity building. In simplest terms, this could be framed as "trust the process," meaning there needs to be a structured process that guides teachers and principals with support from district leaders in the continuous improvement of teaching and learning. And when district and school leaders serve as role models of these processes and behaviors, the improvement of practice is 5.3 times more likely to be successful (Bachmann et al., 2021). In LBUSD this is known by all as The Long Beach Way. In the work of InnovateEd, this came to be known as a coherent system of continuous improvement. Both have the following key elements:

1. A strategic focus guides the collective efforts of school site staff.

2. Agreed-upon outcomes drive the equitable growth in student learning.

3. Clearly defined student learning priorities inform the design of rigorous and complex student learning tasks.

4. Multiple sources of evidence (data, student work, learning rounds, student interviews, and survey results) monitor the impact of teaching on student learning growth.

5. A robust collaborative inquiry process guides recurring 4- to 6-week cycles of teaching and learning (and at 9 to 12 weeks with school sites and the central office).

What is important to note is the absence of a predefined instructional approach. This is intentional in that the dialog among school staff in defining how best to engage students in the learning process, test this theory of action, and continue to seek better methods for accelerating student learning is the primary purpose of the process. However, the problem of practice often seen among schools and in districts is the prescription of an instructional approach or assessment method followed by an expectation for fidelity to realize gains in student achievement.

This is not continuous improvement but rather Einstein's theory of insanity in action: doing the same thing over again and expecting better results.

The most important insight is that precision of pedagogy and instructional coherence cannot be realized through prescription. An agreed-upon process must, by design, engage teachers and leaders in the work of developing collective expertise by learning how to improve the impact of teaching on student learning, the outcome of which is sustaining equitable growth in student learning and, ultimately, having a common way that staff within a school and school sites within a district co-create a coherent system of continuous improvement.

District and School Story

Having had an opportunity to reflect on the last school site visits, Erin and Jacob both were struggling with how to better understand the promising practices and problems of practice among the four schools. Erin had been struck by how different school sites were in their approach to improving teaching and learning, whereas Jacob was more focused on comparing his school and the others to better understand differences in climate, culture, and capacity. At the end of a principal meeting, they had a few minutes to catch up, and Jacob made a statement that greatly affected Erin's thinking. He rhetorically asked Erin if she believed there was a consistent way among any schools in the district for the improvement of teaching and learning. Her response was that the use of common tools, resources, and practices had been reinforced but was uncertain as to "the way" that schools attended to the work. That quick conversation laid the groundwork for the next site visits, during which they would ask schools to share how they engaged in the continuous improvement of teaching and learning—or more simply what was "their way."

Jacob was interested in learning how schools built capacity to improve teaching and learning, and Erin was focused on understanding the degree to which there was coherence within and among school sites. They agreed to focus on both building capacity and creating coherence and again created a set of questions so that there would be consistency in how each school was asked to share their promising practices and problems of practice.

1. Is there a common vision or purpose that guides the work of all staff in the school?

2. Are there agreed-upon processes at your school that have been effective with building capacity to continuously improve teaching and learning?

3. Is there instructional coherence in your school, and if so, what do you believe has been most critical for this to occur over time?

The principals of the four schools that agreed to be visited had asked to receive the questions in advance of this third visit. Clearly, school staff had come to understand that Erin and Jacob had a set of questions and now wanted to be better prepared for the visit. Erin was a little reluctant to share the questions in advance for fear that there would be too much preparation and less authenticity in the dialog. Jacob was less apprehensive because his staff wanted to know what he was looking for in classroom visits, and it was only fair to communicate in advance what information they were seeking for the school sites. First up again was the school that had been noted on the previous charts as "compliant" with district goals and expectations. Upon entering the room, the principal frontloaded the conversation in sharing that the questions received were general and not connected to any guidance provided by the district in the past. Erin, feeling compelled to respond, asked the principal and teachers to further share their thoughts and insights on the lack of district guidance. Before anyone spoke, Jacob noticed three phrases on the whiteboard: common purpose, capacity building process, and instructional coherence. And so he subtly asked if these phrases had been discussed prior to the visit, assuming that this was the case. A teacher spoke and explained that these phrases had been written to simplify the questions that had been shared, and that their intention was to expand upon these, but they had not gotten too far. Erin then asked a great question, "Why do you think this was somewhat of a challenging task?" The senior-most teacher, who shared she was retiring at the end of the year, blatantly stated, "Because we don't have any of these in place at our school." Seeing such candor from a teacher, Erin felt some

(Continued)

(Continued)

level of responsibility to engage and asked how the district could
be more supportive and helpful in this regard, at which point most
staff openly shared their thoughts and ideas, which all related to a
common theme: stop telling schools what to do to improve, and
start working with schools so they can understand how to improve.
Toward the end of the meeting, Jacob brought the group back
together with a final question, "If I'm understanding correctly,
your staff values the three phrases on the board and wants to
be supported in a way that helps you put these into action at
your school?" The soon-to-retire teacher spoke for the group
and stated that she wouldn't be so eager to retire if these were
already in place at the school. In leaving the room, Erin shared
a final thought with the group: "Where there's a will, there's a
way. And I look forward to better supporting your improvement
efforts." When they had left the room, Jacob commended Erin
for her gracious words and noted that there was a desire but a
lack of capacity at the school. And that what was thought of as
compliance now seemed to point to the need for a better district
model for building the capacity of schools. Erin left the school
wondering if, in the absence of school capacity, the default would
be a compliance orientation to the central office. Do some schools
simply comply with district directives when they don't understand
what to do and how to do it?

Upon entering the parking lot of the next school, which was
considered to be "prescriptive" in approach to teaching and
learning, there was a feeling of anxiety between Jacob and
Erin as to how staff would react to the questions provided to
them. Jacob shared with Erin that he thought the school could
be confrontational because the questions may be perceived
as evaluative and judgmental in nature. They both entered the
room expecting to be faced with a tough crowd. But to their
surprise, they were openly welcomed and handed a portfolio
of documents that the staff had prepared for the visit. The
principal started off the meeting with a sense of exuberance as
the portfolio contents were unveiled. What was inside were the
original documents created by the principal and staff that had
guided them in opening the school many years ago. The school
mission and vision, guiding principles, instructional framework,
and agreed-upon school practices were all within the folder.

Jacob was impressed and asked the staff to share more of how these documents were helpful in moving the school forward. What was explained felt more like the story of the school from inception and a description of what the school was intended to be in the minds of those who opened it years ago. The principal chimed in that this packet was given to all new staff members and was shared with parents who wanted to know more about the school. There was definitely a sense of pride among school staff in how these documents described a high-performing school. Erin knew that the student demographics had been changing since the opening of the school and so asked whether staff had considered if these documents needed updating to reflect the current student population. The principal was quick to state, "No. This is who we are and what we do. These documents are the foundation of our success," after which, all teachers nodded their heads in agreement. Jacob then asked, "But how do you know what worked in the past will be equally as effective in the future?" This time Erin was the one to sense a feeling of judgment from Jacob's question and so reframed it by asking, "I think what we're asking is, how does your school continuously improve teaching and learning?" A teacher quite boldly stated that the documents that had been shared describe how the school supports student learning. Another teacher referenced the page that listed school-wide practices. Jacob then directly asked this teacher whether she felt there were any changes that might be needed to this page. The answer was a steadfast, "No, I don't." Erin and Jacob politely thanked the staff for sharing their documents and expressed appreciation for their time and learning more about their school. When debriefing in the car, the common perception was that the school was not prescriptive in nature but actually resistant to changing what was perceived to be the perfect school. The mission and vision of the school was more important than student learning needs. The school had a way not for continuously improving but rather maintaining a strong sense of school pride. Jacob made a side comment to Erin, "Good is the enemy of great."

Prior to visiting the next school that had been identified as "fragmented," Erin thought it best to call the principal in

(Continued)

(Continued)

advance. She was elated to hear that the last visit had in fact
initiated productive conversations among staff about shared
leadership and that the principal did want to see how this next
visit might also provide the same type of questioning coupled
with support and guidance. Erin suggested that the meeting
be led by the principal to engage the staff in sharing and that
she and Jacob would shape ideas for consideration as the
sharing progressed. Upon entering the room at the school
site, it was clear that the principal had set the meeting up
as Erin suggested. The questions were written on the board,
teachers were seated in a half-circle all facing the board, and
Jacob and Erin were positioned between the board and the
staff. Jacob jokingly commented, "This feels like we're being
interviewed," as he took a seat in the half-circle facing the staff.
The principal commented that this structure would allow staff
to see the questions and at the same time engage in dialog
with each other and with their visitors and then commenced to
read each question and give time and opportunity for staff to
share insights and listen to comments and questions from Erin
and Jacob. But what transpired was individuals, and at times
a few members, advocating for their own perspectives rather
than listening to and building upon each other's thoughts. It
felt disjointed and almost confrontational in how staff members
were stating their positions and expecting conformity of others
to their thinking. After about 15 minutes of this unproductive
interaction among staff members, Jacob asked a question:
"Why does it feel like you're advocating for others to agree
with you rather than having a common way of describing
your purpose, processes, and practices?" There was a long
moment of silence, and then one of the newer teachers stated
he had not heard the staff having conversations about these
topics before and assumed that the group was going through
what he was taught in his credentialing program as "storming
and norming." A few of the teachers did not appreciate his
comment, but others seemed to agree with him. So Erin asked
another question, "How does the staff at your school engage
in the continuous improvement of teaching and learning?" One
of the teachers who seemed a little disgruntled commented
that most of the school staff had been teaching for 20 or more

years and that each had their own way of approaching teaching and learning. The principal, who was waiting for an opportunity to prompt productive dialog, asked whether the expertise among staff could be shared in a way that may result in a few commonly agreed-upon ways of supporting student learning. The staff seemed to be responsive, and so the principal moved to the whiteboard and began asking each teacher to share their ideas for charting. After a long list had been generated, the principal then wrote on the board three headers—common purpose, common processes, and common practices—and asked the staff to assist with grouping ideas under each heading. At this point, Erin and Jacob thanked the staff for the opportunity to visit and exited the room. Erin commented that like the compliant school, the fragmented school seemed willing to engage in the work and yet needed some type of structure and guidance for the conversations to unfold. Jacob agreed and wondered who was learning more from these visits: Erin and him or the schools themselves.

Erin and Jacob received an email from the principal of the last school to be visited. They were intrigued about meeting this staff, because the school had already shown to have coherence, but were dismayed when the email indicated that the meeting would be replaced by classroom visits. Upon meeting the principal at the school office, Erin asked why there was a change in plans. The principal shared that after reading the questions, the staff thought it best to see teaching and learning in action rather than hearing it described in a meeting. And then the principal shared a document that was titled "Instructional Rounds," which had a brief description of teaching and learning practices at the school, and asked Jacob and Erin what they would like to focus on while visiting classrooms. Jacob asked whether this was created for the visit today, and in fact it had not, but was created by the school leadership team earlier in the year. The staff wanted to have a few priorities to focus their collaboration and instructional planning. Erin was intrigued and asked, "Why did the staff want to have this, and how did they come together to create it?" The principal explained that because she had been visiting classrooms regularly, the staff wanted to have input on what she could expect to see happening in classrooms, and so they created what might be

(Continued)

(Continued)

called teaching and learning practices. The previous principal had the book *Instructional Rounds* on a shelf, and the staff had been given the book but had never read it. So there was a book study, and the staff liked the concept of the "instructional core": student tasks encircled by student engagement, content rigor, and teacher expertise. The document was intended to describe what would be seen as students engaged in rigorous learning tasks with instructional support from teachers. Jacob, in thinking about the last school visit asked, "So does this define the purpose, process, and practices of your school?" The principal had not considered this schema but implied that the document seemed to do just that. The trio spent an hour visiting classrooms and using the document to discuss what was seen and share insights about teaching and learning in each classroom. Before leaving the school, Erin asked Jacob and the school principal if they thought this would be a valuable process for all principals to experience. The response was a resounding affirmative. In fact, Jacob went a little further in stating that this would help develop capacity and create coherence among principals and school sites. Erin asked the principal if, when an opportunity arose, she would be willing to share this document and process with her peers. She agreed but clearly was a little anxious about this possibility.

The next afternoon Jacob met with Erin in her office to debrief the school visits. She had already laid out the charts from the previous two visits and had on the whiteboard a chart for capturing key ideas from their observations that focused on capacity building and creating coherence (Figure 4.1). She had changed the "prescriptive" school to be labeled "resistant," and Jacob inferred this meant resistant to change. Three big ideas were also listed on the whiteboard: common purpose, agreed-upon process for improving teaching and learning, and instructional coherence. Jacob inquired whether they would use the same process of using sticky notes to capture ideas and then combine into final comments to write in the chart. Erin agreed, and the two spent several hours writing comments and wordsmithing content to be charted. When finished, each took some time to read through their collective efforts.

Figure 4.1	Key Indicators of School Capacity and Coherence			
SCHOOL PROFILE	**CAPACITY BUILDING**	**INSTRUCTIONAL COHERENCE**	**IMPACT ON SCHOOL IMPROVEMENT**	**QUESTIONS TO BE CONSIDERED**
Compliant	Staff does not have an agreed-upon process that guides the improvement of teaching and learning.	Staff does not engage in sharing of best practices to develop a common set of practices.	Staff has not yet developed capacity to co-lead the ongoing improvement of school practices.	How can the school best be supported to further develop capacity of staff with creating coherence?
Resistant	Staff is comfortable with the status quo and resistant to the changing of current school practices.	Staff desires to maintain autonomy by connecting the work of individuals to a static school mission and vision.	Staff appreciates school pride more than improving practices to meet the learning needs of all students.	How can the school come to understand that continuous improvement is critical for achieving long-term success?
Fragmented	Staff do not have common beliefs or agreements as to how best to support student learning.	Staff are willing to create a common set of practices but lack clear norms and a process to do so.	Staff do not yet value the concept of working together to get better together.	In what ways can staff be engaged in structured processes to build capacity and create coherence?
Coherent	Staff have commonly agreed-upon tools and processes that guide improvement of school practices.	Staff are open to working together and co-learning new ways for improving teaching and learning.	The school has a collaborative inquiry process that is used by all for continuous improvement.	What has had the most impact with building the capacity of staff to create school coherence?

© 2022 InnovateEd

(Continued)

(Continued)

Jacob suggested that because their questions for consideration were focused on better understanding how to support schools, it was important to share their findings with school principals. He was becoming uncomfortable with what could become predefining school site supports without input or feedback from principals. Erin disagreed because she saw this as action research and not for the purpose of designing central office supports for school sites. Her suggestion was that student data sets created by her office would be provided at the next principal meeting and that a final school visit could serve as a way to learn how school sites utilize this evidence. Jacob was accustomed to receiving these quarterly data reports and was also interested in seeing how schools used this information. So both agreed that the last school visits would focus on how evidence of student learning was utilized by the staff of each school.

Creating Instructional Coherence

Creating instructional coherence is not realized by disseminating tools and resources that delineate learning priorities, instructional practices, and student outcomes. Rather, it is an ongoing process for improving the instructional core, that is, maintaining high levels of student engagement in the learning of rigorous and complex learning tasks supported by teachers with pedagogical expertise (City et al., 2009). Successfully engaging students in rigorous and complex tasks calls upon teachers to integrate curricular resources with instructional strategies and assessments for learning in a way that supports the learning needs of all students. This is realized when school sites, in collaboration with district staff, design and refine guiding principles for high-quality instruction that improves student learning at the classroom desk. This ongoing interaction and co-learning ensures that a coherent instructional framework will evolve in depth and specificity as precision of practices within and among schools strengthens the instructional core. Creating instructional coherence does not have an end point but is an agile improvement process driven by the moral imperative of student equity.

This can be a challenging endeavor because a common approach for schools and districts is to guide teaching and learning with commonly accessible standards-aligned resources. Some may think of this as a

> Creating instructional coherence does not have an end point but is an agile improvement process driven by the moral imperative of student equity.

pacing guide, others may consider this as an assessment framework, and a few default to using adopted materials verbatim for such guidance. Instructional coherence is not the same as alignment with or fidelity to predefined instructional resources. These mindsets are akin to the former era of standards-based materials that were designed to reduce variation in teaching and learning that exists within schools and, even more so, across school districts. If one were to consider the differences that exist among schools, such as teacher tenure, student demographics, and school climate and culture, then it becomes immediately clear that such top-down guidance will not result in equitable improvement of student learning. In reality, the determining factor is whether school staff have the collective capacity to maximize the impact of these instructional resources and strategies for achieving equitable growth in student learning. It is not what resources you have, rather it is how you use the resources that matters most.

An example of this work in action was noted in *Districts on the Move* through the story of Little Lake City School District. This school district had spent years aligning instructional resources and tools that guided teaching and learning. This centralized approach was appreciated by teachers and principals because it had created instructional coherence among school sites. The central office and principals had grown a little skeptical of this long-standing top-down approach and were interested in further developing the capacity of school sites to take the reins on improving teaching and learning. This shift in creating instructional coherence from that of district-focused to site-driven was precarious at first because schools began to question the impact and effectiveness of district-wide resources and strategies. The focus on student learning at the classroom desk with a sharp lens on the instructional core began to further flush out equity issues among students. The work occurring within schools and among teachers and principals began to have more influence on the improvement of district-wide instructional tools and resources. After a few years, schools had become even wiser consumers and more active curators of the resources used for engaging students in learning at the classroom desk. So it is not an either-or process for creating instructional coherence, rather it's the beauty of and, meaning that instructional coherence requires both instructional tools and resources and the capacity of school sites to engage in the ongoing process of developing specificity and precision in how these materials are used to meet the learning needs of all students. And because new students arrive every year, and each school experiences shifts in teachers and principals, instructional coherence has to continuously be revisited, adapted, and modified to accommodate these recurring changes.

Within a given school site, creating instructional coherence can take root from several starting points. There could be a pacing guide, adopted instructional materials, an assessment platform, or a predefined instructional model for at-risk students that has been given to or acquired by a school. These tools and resources may or may not be appreciated or used effectively by staff. Again, tools and resources in of themselves do not create instructional coherence. When school staff begin to focus on the impact of learning at the classroom desk, student equity issues will become clearer. And this will create a need or demand for inquiring how to maximize the impact of these tools and resources on student learning growth. At this point there will be either a sense of frustration or an opportunity to adapt and refine how teaching and learning are approached. Those schools that delve into fine-tuning the use of tools and resources to discern how to maximize the impact on student learning will inevitably engage in the process of creating instructional coherence. Those who remain frustrated will ultimately seek out new and different tools and resources that will result in the vicious cycle of seeking a "silver bullet" for improving teaching and learning. The former will take the long road of creating instructional coherence, and the latter will succumb to a reliance on tools and materials to guide teaching and learning. The desired outcome is that school teachers, in collaboration with site principals with district support, engage in the ongoing processes of learning how to maximize the impact of teaching on student learning by developing precision of practices. And when this occurs among all staff in a school or preferably among all schools within a district, the result will be the creation of an agreed-upon instructional framework that guides teaching and learning.

Creating Instructional Coherence in LBUSD

To ensure instructional coherence and build the capacity of instructional teams, LBUSD adopted system-, school-, and classroom-level practices to bring about equitable outcomes for a diverse student population. The most robust processes are at the system level. Instructional experts from LBUSD and staff from California State University Long Beach meet on a regular basis to review preservice courses for incoming teachers to ensure that individuals receive research-based instructional practices that align to the equity-driven work of the school system. The LBUSD Office of Curriculum and Instruction and Professional Development and Research brings teachers together over the summer to refine and/or develop common assessments in all subject areas at all grade levels to be deployed the following school year. The LBUSD Research department provides numerous professional learning opportunities for teachers and site administrators on how to develop their own classroom assessments and evaluate data to enhance student learning.

In addition, the LBUSD Instructional Steering Committee meets monthly to collaborate and analyze findings from CIV/quarterly visits to refine support provided to schools from the central office. Those schools, identified as Focus Schools through this process, are supported by central office instructional support personnel to provide professional learning support to teachers and administrators based on the problem of practice identified by individual school sites. The executive cabinet meets weekly to discuss instructional needs of the schools and make modifications in central office support systems. This allows for real-time allocation of fiscal resources to support specific student interventions that need to be implemented based on data from the CIV/quarterly visits. To promote transparency of improvement efforts, the Board of Education is provided two opportunities each year to take field trips to schools and attend professional learning sessions to see firsthand how the school system is addressing equitable outcomes for students.

At the school level, all new administrators are provided a coach to build capacity with leading the LBUSD improvement process. All monthly administrator meetings have an instructional focus, which is to ensure that site administrators spend 50% of their time in classrooms supporting the continuous improvement efforts of the school. Sites record how many visits each administrator makes to classrooms on a monthly basis and reports this data to their supervisor. In addition, instructional leadership teams from each site are brought together twice a year for a full day of learning and collaboration to address the instructional needs of all students. And at the classroom level, all new teachers receive 2 years of coaching from district personnel who are experts in a particular grade level and/or content area. All teachers are provided numerous paid professional development opportunities to enhance their skills as teachers. Some of these sessions are required by the system, whereas others are preselected by the teacher based on their own professional growth.

Fostering Robust Collaborative Inquiry Processes

Creating instructional coherence has been described as a collaborative inquiry process that over time develops the capacity and expertise of school staff to engage students in rigorous and complex tasks with high-impact instructional supports. A robust collaborative inquiry process is essential for creating instructional coherence. The best way to frame this process is through recurring 3- to 4-week instructional cycles guided by an instructional framework that informs how school staff attend to teaching and learning. Within such a cycle are the four phases of analyze, design, implement, and refine. Analyze student learning needs to define instructional priorities that focus efforts on overcoming the identified problems of practice for teaching and learning. Design instructional approaches and learning outcomes that will inform the student learning process. Implement these instructional practices and student supports while making adjustments based on evidence of impact on student learning. Refine the teaching and learning process informed by a common understanding of what works best and why that has been discerned through the analysis of student learning progress and growth. This is the collaborative inquiry process that creates instructional coherence and develops precision of pedagogy.

The challenge is that this collaborative inquiry approach in many cases has not been fully developed or effectively supported to guide the work of school staff or the efforts of schools within a district. To do so requires that district and school leaders foster a robust collaborative inquiry process. And when we say foster, this is not the same defining, prescribing, or expecting collaborative inquiry to occur within and among school sites. It cannot be assumed that inquiry will be the primary driver of teacher collaboration during Wednesday professional learning community (PLC) time. Providing school staff with dedicated time, instructional tools and resources, and access to student learning evidence will not result in the precision of practice that maximizes impact on student learning. There must be a structured process that guides the co-learning and co-leading of school improvement efforts. And fostering such a process requires that leaders have strategies for encouraging, promoting, and developing capacity of school staff. This is a high-level investment of time and energy among district and school leaders. And the old adage of "what is calendared gets done" should be top of mind. So the question to consider is, how much time and energy do leaders expend on fostering collaborative inquiry?

Mary Jean Gallagher has described her experience with fostering collaborative inquiry when serving as superintendent of schools in Ontario, Canada. She understood the value of collaborative inquiry and wanted the district leaders to become more proactive in fostering this among school sites. And so she had asked her district staff to engage school sites through an inquiry stance to assist with guiding their improvement efforts. When asked to share the progress of such visits, most all administrators noted the lack of time to do so. In the end, Mary Jean required that no district leaders were to be in their offices on Wednesdays and instead needed to be at school sites engaged in collaborative inquiry with school leaders and staff. Only then did the modeling and nurturing of an inquiry process begin to take root at the district and school site levels. As noted, what gets calendared is what gets accomplished.

Chris Steinhauser has a similar story of how the work unfolded in LBUSD. District leaders and site principals had established a collaborative inquiry visitation process every 9 weeks at secondary schools and 12 weeks at elementary schools. This took shape as both an ending and a beginning of a collaborative inquiry cycle, sharing progress of improvement efforts to clarify promising practices and analyzing evidence of impact to focus direction on overcoming newly identified problems of practice. In the interim of visits, school sites engaged in the phases of designing improvement strategies and then implementing and adjusting based on the evidence of impact on student learning. Schools were paired or grouped based on similar problems of practice and were visited by a team of district leaders. And so this became a true district and school collaborative inquiry endeavor that occurred every 9 to 12 weeks among all school sites. That is a high level of commitment to the ongoing process of encouraging, promoting, and developing a robust collaborative inquiry process.

The InnovateEd team has witnessed school sites in the absence of a district-wide model engage in the development of a collaborative inquiry process for improving teaching and learning. Corona-Norco USD had an approach that was more of an opt-in opportunity for school sites. Support was provided to opt-in schools in the form of school leadership team development supported by InnovateEd. This was designed as four to six sessions per year over a 2-year period to assist school sites with engaging in collaborative inquiry cycles and, over time, developing internal capacity to sustain the improvement process. Many school sites connected three to five sequential PLC Wednesdays to construct a collaborative inquiry cycle and then engaged in recurring cycles of analyze, design, implement, and refine every 4 to 6 weeks to develop capacity of teacher teams to co-lead collaborative inquiry. These schools were effective in their ability to develop an internal process for continuous improvement and share their progress and impact with other sites for an organic approach to creating systemic collaborative inquiry within the district. This would be more akin to the theory of action for scaling high-impact practices through a diffusion of innovation model.

The catalyst of change can begin at the teacher level as often occurs within schools when one or more teacher teams work together in a way that develops a robust collaborative inquiry process. These teachers plan instruction, discuss instructional approaches, analyze evidence of student learning, and create common agreements for engaging students in the learning process. At some point, their efforts become noticed by the site principal, who begins to more actively support their improvement processes. And slowly over time, more teachers and teams begin to engage in similar processes until there becomes a commonly agreed-upon process for engaging in collaborative inquiry. Then through principal dialog, the work of the school becomes known to other sites and begins to shape and influence how other schools attend to the process of improving teaching and learning. Hopefully there is a district leader who seizes upon the opportunity to foster more robust collaborative inquiry processes among all school sites. Never dismiss the power of how a few teachers can influence the work in their own school and potentially affect how the district attends to the continuous improvement of teaching and learning.

Fostering robust collaborative inquiry processes can be initiated by the central office, co-constructed with district leaders and site principals, taken on by individual schools with a system of support, or even be driven by the collective commitment of a few individuals within a school site. Ultimately, the approach taken is dependent on the culture of the school district and the capacity of school sites to co-lead improvement efforts. What is most essential for consideration is how school and district leaders can best nurture, promote, and develop an agreed-upon collaborative inquiry cycle that improves teaching and learning. And this does require dedicated time, energy, and focus among school principals and staff and some form of ongoing support from district leaders to sustain these recurring instructional cycles and improvement processes.

Developing Precision of Pedagogy

Pedagogy is the study of how knowledge and skills are exchanged during the learning process through interactions that take place between the teacher and students and among students. This differs from instructional strategies that are methods for engaging students in the learning process. A way to better understand this difference is to consider the book *Classroom Instruction That Works* (Marzano, 2001), which references nine research-based instructional strategies. At a conference the audience was asked how many knew of this work, and almost all raised their hands. Those with hands raised were asked to keep them in the air if they were able to name the nine strategies, and many hands went down. Then those with hands still raised were asked if they remembered reading Chapter 12, which described how to effectively plan instruction and implement these strategies. At this point there were no longer any hands in the air. Most knew of the strategies, few could explicitly name them, and none could describe how to use them effectively. This is the difference between having knowledge of an instructional strategy versus the precision of pedagogy for actively engaging students in the learning process. Some would go as far as to say that many schools are strategy rich and yet learning poor.

John Hattie has encountered similar circumstances when several years ago he was the keynote for a large conference of education leaders in California, at which time he commented to the audience that his visible learning research had been done to delineate the most effective instructional strategies and practices in education. And yet schools and districts had not put this research into practice to improve teaching and learning. This brings to light a common dilemma in education in that the research is accessible, but the research has not had the desired impact on how learning occurs within schools and classrooms. What if the solution was not for educators to be better consumers of research but for educators to become better action researchers? What if educational research was not the end goal but instead a starting point from which to engage in collaborative inquiry and seek out better methods of teaching and learning that resulted in precision of pedagogy? So maybe we're asking educators the wrong question. Rather than asking, "How are you using research-based practices?" we should be asking, "What action research have you done that has provided clarity for maximizing the impact of teaching on student learning?" When reframed in this manner, developing precision of pedagogy is achieved through a robust collaborative inquiry process that engages teachers and administrators within a school to learn how to ensure all students demonstrate growth in learning. It is student equity in action.

Developing precision of pedagogy is achieved through a robust collaborative inquiry process that engages teachers and administrators within a school to learn how to ensure all students demonstrate growth in learning.

As has already been noted, collaborative inquiry is a four-phase process of analyzing evidence to prioritize the focus of teaching and learning, designing high-impact instructional approaches with evidence to inform the teaching and learning process, implementing strategies and adjusting based on the impact on student learning, and analyzing evidence of the impact on student learning growth to refine teaching and learning practices by collectively understanding what works best and why. Evidence of student learning is a common denominator of all four phases and is in fact the key driver of action research and continuous improvement. There are five sources of evidence that should be considered in the process of developing precision of pedagogy: formative assessment data, student work, learning rounds (i.e., observing the learning process in classrooms), student interviews, and survey results. These sources of evidence are used to triangulate multiple sources of information for the purpose of clearly discerning the barriers of and solutions for improving the impact of teaching on student learning. The foundational sources of evidence are data, student work, and learning rounds because all are directly connected to student learning at the classroom desk. The added value sources of evidence are survey results and student interviews because both are a powerful means from which to better understand the perspectives of students, staff, and parents.

This collaborative inquiry process for developing precision of pedagogy might play out as follows within a school. During the analyze phase, student data disaggregated by student groups, ethnicity, and gender are analyzed to develop a deeper understanding of the problems of practices that are barriers to student learning growth. Student work samples may also be analyzed to gain a deeper perspective of the strengths and constraints among students with use of specific skills. With this information in hand, a theory of action and clear strategies of how to approach teaching and learning is designed. And evidence of learning is agreed upon for monitoring student progress, which would consist of student work and learning rounds focused on specific student attributes and outcomes. Teaching and learning practices would then be implemented during which time the information gathered from student work and learning rounds would inform adjustments to teaching and learning practices. At the conclusion of the collaborative inquiry cycle, student interviews and survey results may, and formative assessment data certainly would, be analyzed to make informed decisions as to how best to refine teaching and learning moving forward. This process could be attended to by the school leadership team in addition to some or all teacher teams at the school. Optimally, site administrators would be engaged in the process as well as district staff in a supportive and co-learning role.

What has been described could be considered as the "gold standard" for engaging in a robust collaborative inquiry process that develops precision of pedagogy. The intention is not to advocate that schools rush into such a process but, rather, slowly embark on the journey of building capacity to continuously improve teaching and learning. Therefore it is essential to take into account school climate (beliefs), culture (behaviors), capacity (efficacy), and coherence (shared depth of understanding). Do school staff have an appreciation of or a common approach for co-leading a collaborative inquiry process? Do school staff have an affinity for analyzing multiple sources of student learning evidence, or is there a sense of trepidation or even resistance? Do school staff desire to refine teaching and learning and achieve more equitable growth in student learning, or is there comfortability with the status quo or fear of change? All these questions and more must be considered because the key to success is not the speed of execution but achieving small successes that create momentum for attending to more difficult challenges.

As can be imagined, developing precision of pedagogy is a never-ending process because there will always be year-to-year changes in the students within classrooms as well as the fact that increased staff expertise leads to deeper understanding of student learning needs. The aforementioned collaborative inquiry process should be thought of as recurring instructional cycles that align with periods of time (i.e., 4 to 6 weeks) or connect to units of study with clear priorities and outcomes for student learning. The intent is not to be precise with pedagogy for a fixed time but rather to develop a common understanding of how to maximize the impact of instructional practices on student learning growth. This moves away from what some might consider as content-based expertise toward that of learning-centered expertise: how to ensure that all students demonstrate the ability to complete rigorous and complex tasks by applying key cognitive skills as part of the learning process. In *Districts on the Move* we had referred to these key cognitive skills as visible evidence of student learning (see Figure 4.2). And this framework of student learning evidence can serve as a guide for school sites that focuses efforts on ensuring all students demonstrate these critical skills.

Figure 4.2 Visible Evidence of Student Learning	
Higher-Order Thinking Skills Students engage in rigorous and complex tasks requiring analysis, reasoning, evaluation, logic, problem-solving, justifying, and transferring learning to new contexts via planning and creativity.	**Close and Analytic Reading** Students access and interpret media types with a clear purpose requiring annotation, source-dependent questions, notetaking, and analysis of information to gain knowledge for engaging in evidence-based conversations, writing, and performance tasks.
Precise Use of Rigorous Academic Language Students speak and write with precise use of general academic and domain-specific vocabulary, grammar, syntax, and word meaning as part of productive discourse related to content-specific subject matter.	**Structured Student Collaboration** Students effectively work in pairs or groups on clearly defined tasks with specific roles and responsibilities for engaging in structured academic discourse to convey understanding, share ideas, and build upon the thoughts and reasoning of others.
Evidence-Based Arguments Students develop claims, conjectures, and hypotheses that require analysis of information and interpretation of evidence to construct meaning, apply reasoning, and justify the logic of models.	**Evidence-Based Writing** Students clearly communicate through short constructed responses and process writing across content areas for a variety of purposes and audiences to justify opinions and arguments with evidence, show understanding of concepts, and transfer learning to new contexts.

© 2022 InnovateEd

To this end, an inquiry question that can sustain the continuous improvement of teaching and learning could be framed like this: "I wonder how we can further improve teaching and learning so that all students demonstrate equal levels of success in applying key cognitive skills to complete rigorous and complex learning tasks?" In doing so, schools clearly define the purpose and focus of developing precision of pedagogy: equitable growth in student learning. For the purpose of teaching and learning is not to achieve an outcome but rather to ensure all students have the key cognitive skills to effectively engage in and have ownership of the learning process. Precision of pedagogy should be focused on deepening student learning.

The Path of Progress for Holmes Elementary School

Lori Grady is the principal of Holmes Elementary School in Long Beach. She has been at the site for 3 years after having served as principal at several other schools as well as an administrator at the central office. Upon arrival at the site, it was clear that school staff had a deeply held belief that all students can learn at high levels, and student achievement results demonstrated that teachers were positively affecting student learning growth. The keys to this success were seen as the relationships between staff and students and the willingness of staff to figure out how best to support the learning of all students. At the heart of this was a student learning profile that aligned instruction with student learning interests and needs. This could be framed as a personalized instructional approach for engaging students in meaningful learning opportunities. The school had a student-centered culture in which teachers served as facilitators of learning. An emphasis was placed on high levels of student engagement with personalized learning tasks supported by differentiated instruction. As principal, Lori's role would be to promote and nurture this culture of collaboration and equity-driven improvement.

This deep level of instructional capacity and coherence existed in spite of serving a diverse student population ranging from poverty to upper middle-class families. A culture of collaborative inquiry driven by continuous improvement ensured that barriers to student learning growth were overcome by school staff. Although the school staff developed theories of action through the analysis of data and planning of instructional units to meet student learning needs, this was seen as a normal expectation that staff surpassed by personalizing and differentiating instruction to actively engage students in their own learning. In this regard, the three priorities in the school became creating a positive learning environment, increasing student engagement, and differentiating instruction. As the pandemic unfolded, and the school shifted to remote learning, the staff worked tirelessly to ensure that students had access to the materials and resources needed for a high-quality learning environment. Maintaining a strong connection with students was a top priority for school staff, who were open to asking students how they wanted to engage in learning, which was not diminished even though teaching and learning had changed dramatically.

Because the staff had experienced the positive impact of their work on student learning growth, a culture of risk-taking was instilled that drove the continuous improvement of teaching and learning. In this regard, district resources were only a guide that informed teaching and learning in a nonprescriptive manner. The staff at Holmes Elementary School has taken the helm with guiding teaching and learning in a way that increases student engagement and achieves growth in student learning. The loose-tight relationship between the central office and school sites has been critical for the development of the culture and practices within the school site. There is a true balance of structure and autonomy in relation to central office expectations and school site action steps. The outside-of-the-box thinking among staff to discover how to best engage students in learning based on their needs and interests is what makes Holmes Elementary School a school on the move. The challenge for Lori and the staff is maintaining and sustaining the positive impact of school improvement efforts.

The Path of Progress for Lakeside Middle School

Little Lake City School District, a K–8 school district in California, had been a case study for *Districts on the Move* to highlight how to create clarity of district goals and school priorities for student learning. Over a 3-year period of time, district leaders, site principals, and school teachers had shifted from a district improvement model to a site-driven improvement process. The use of school action plans and an agreed-upon collaborative inquiry process ensured that improvement efforts focused on ensuring all students successfully completed rigorous and complex learning tasks to achieve equitable growth in student learning. One of the school sites, Lakeside Middle School, continued down this path of progress to develop even more depth and precision of school-wide instructional practices.

These continued improvement efforts began when the school principal, Ana Gutierrez, wondered how collaboration among content and grade-level teams could be expanded upon to further accelerate student learning. The school already had an action plan that guided 9-week improvement cycles with clearly delineated strategies for teaching and learning. Staff analyzed data and collaboratively planned instruction as grade-level and content area teams. But the focus was not on identifying and overcoming the learning gaps that existed among individual students. The staff agreed to integrate school-wide collaboration time as part of the collaboration model wherein samples of student work would be dissected to identify trends and patterns among all grade levels and content areas. This allowed the staff to have a "balcony" view of student learning progress that provided many insights as to the learning gaps among students. The key question was: "What are successful students able to do and demonstrate that unsuccessful students have not yet developed the skills and abilities to do so also?"

Over time, the staff transitioned to creating index cards for each student in the school that described their academic performance and learning needs. This allowed the analysis of student work to go deeper with analyzing the specific learning needs of individual students and student groups. As staff worked together to define the problems of practice among students, the initial conversations were superficial (i.e., better readers or more involved parents) and then became more specific as to the actual learning challenges occurring among students. These efforts were led by the school leadership team with support from Ana in her lead learner role as principal. A protocol for student work analysis was created to focus the dialog on identifying learning gaps and clarifying the instructional supports for overcoming learning barriers. Eventually student work was being analyzed across content area teams so that student learning challenges could be seen not as a content challenge but rather connected to the cognitive skills students applied during the learning process.

This led to the conversations among staff to shift from identifying successful and struggling students to clarifying successful instructional strategies and making agreements as to school-wide instructional practices. One example was the realization a root cause of student literacy gaps was the fragmented use of nonlinguistic representations between grade levels and content areas. Essentially students were learning and relearning how to utilize these academic language support systems within their classes and also between grade levels. The staff recognized a need to determine the best practices for using nonlinguistic representations and come to agreements as to how to do so consistently within content areas and grade levels. Student learning needs guided the refinement and improved precision of school-wide instructional practices. Staff collaboration now focus on the subtle nuances of instructional practices that make a difference in supporting student learning. In the past this would not have been the dialog among teachers, but it has now become the culture of the school.

Tips and Tools for Taking Action

Having supported the improvement efforts of school districts for almost 20 years, Jay has come to recognize a troubling pattern in this work. School districts and sites default to purchasing adopted instructional materials, ascribe to the use of specific research-based instructional strategies, define how students should be assessed, and then require the monitoring of student learning progress at predefined time periods. This would be defined by many school districts as creating instructional coherence to develop precision of pedagogy. Knowing that Long Beach is recognized for high-quality teaching and learning and equitable growth in student learning outcomes, Jay inquired how the approach taken by Long Beach may differ in practice. Chris's response was enlightening in that the curricular resources, instructional strategies, and assessment practices are available and yet optional for all school sites. The primary driver is not fidelity to district-wide tools and resources, rather it is the robust collaborative inquiry processes led by school site teachers and leaders that create instructional coherence and develop precision of pedagogy. If a school site is struggling with improving student learning, then most certainly there are district-level interventions and supports provided to the site. But for the majority of schools, there exists defined autonomy that empowers teachers and leaders to clarify how best to achieve equitable growth in student learning outcomes.

This approach to developing collective expertise is paradoxical. It implies that the school district may provide tools and resources that inform teaching and learning, but these are not mandated or prescribed for use by schools. Instead, sites have the discretion and autonomy to create instructional coherence and develop precision of pedagogy through the process of learning together how best to improve student learning. Continuously improving teaching and learning is the primary driver for school sites to create collective expertise. What follows for those ready to embark on this journey of site-driven capacity building are tips and suggestions that will help accelerate school improvement efforts.

Creating Instructional Coherence

A typical scenario for schools is to participate in a 2-day training on newly adopted materials, acquire an updated standards-based pacing guide, attend a session on how to use the latest assessment platform, receive professional development and a companion book on an instructional approach, and then be left to discern how to effectively use these tools and resources to meet the learning needs of a diverse group of students. This is not a one-time experience; rather, for many teachers and site leaders, this occurs to some extent on an annual basis. And then there is the expectation for school sites to create instructional coherence even though the tools and resources at hand continually shift based on the ongoing changes occurring at the district and state levels. The only viable solution is to create a coherent instructional framework that is not dependent upon the tools and resources at disposal but instead comprises guiding principles that inform high-quality teaching and learning.

Such guiding principles always connect to what Richard Elmore has defined as the instructional core: maintaining high levels of student engagement in the learning of rigorous and complex learning tasks supported by teachers with pedagogical expertise. As we have noted, successfully engaging students in rigorous and complex tasks calls upon teachers to integrate curricular resources with instructional strategies and assessments for learning in a way that supports the learning needs of all students. The goal is to focus the collective efforts of school staff on improving student learning at the classroom desk. Creating instructional coherence is not an outcome but rather an ongoing process of seeking to understand how best to ensure all students successfully complete rigorous and complex learning tasks as part of daily classroom instruction. The first step for school sites to embark on creating collective expertise is establishing guiding principles that can be initially framed as the following essential questions.

1. How can we ensure that all students have equal access to high-quality teaching and learning?

2. How can we integrate curricular resources, instructional strategies, and assessment practices in a way that meets the learning needs of all students?

3. How can we ensure that all students are actively engaged in rigorous and complex learning tasks as part of daily classroom instruction?

4. How can we continuously improve teaching to maximize the impact on student learning?

Fostering Robust Collaborative Inquiry Processes

There is a clear distinction between collaboration that denotes a time, location, and structure for productive group work and that of collaborative inquiry, which is an agreed-upon process for co-learning and co-leading school improvement efforts. For the past 20 years, most school districts have set aside collaboration time for teachers and leaders to plan instruction, assess the impact on student learning, and provide targeted support to struggling students. And yet we do not see the development of collective expertise within most school sites for achieving equitable growth in student learning. The reason for this unfortunate circumstance is that even though school sites have collaboration time, most do not engage in robust collaborative inquiry processes such as lesson study. To shift from a time and structure for collaboration to a process of collaborative inquiry requires that school sites reframe this critical work as teaching and learning cycles. This cannot be a quick change in practice but rather a slow transition that is nurtured and continually reinforced.

At the initial stages, the transition to fostering collaborative inquiry begins as reframing the purpose of collaboration to that of a collaborative inquiry cycle. This usually begins with defining an agreed-upon period of time such as 4 to 6 weeks for which there is a common focus on a problem of practice considered to be a barrier to student learning growth. This could be close and analytical reading, communicating with precise academic language, collaborative student discourse, or using evidence to explain, justify, and defend arguments. Then a theory of action is designed with clearly delineated improvement strategies to be measured with agreed-upon evidence of student learning. Staff work collaboratively to implement the strategies and make adjustments to improve the impact on student learning. At the conclusion of the inquiry cycle, student learning progress and the impact of teaching on student learning is analyzed to discern what works best and why. With these new insights in hand, teachers and leaders refine teaching practices and student learning supports moving into the next cycle. The aforementioned process is attended to in a slow and gradual manner as staff become comfortable and confident with engaging in a robust collaborative inquiry cycle. These efforts must be guided, promoted, and nurtured by site administrators and teacher leaders so that staff have an opportunity to adjust to new ways of working together.

Developing Precision of Pedagogy

When Jay served as an administrator of a county office of education, there were opportunities to visit high-performing school sites that achieved consistent growth in student learning despite teaching underserved student populations. At one such school visit, Jay inquired with the principal as to the secret of the school's long-term success. The answer was that the school focused on only one instructional priority and two instructional strategies each school year. To paraphrase the principal, "We need to become exceptional with teaching and learning, and to do so requires that school staff have a laser-sharp focus." At first this seemed to be too linear of an improvement strategy before it was clear that school staff deeply analyzed the problems of practice among students and uncovered the barriers to student learning growth. The school was in fact developing precision of pedagogy with high-yield instructional strategies to achieve equitable student growth based on a carefully selected learning priority. And so year after year new strategies were selected as different student learning priorities emerged so that over time the staff had developed collective expertise with a multitude of high-yield instructional practices.

This example resembles the adage of Steve Jobs in describing how he turned around the failing company called Apple to become one of the most successful companies in history: simplify and focus. Mary Jean Gallagher, when serving as a senior leader in the Ministry of Education in Ontario, Canada, used such an approach to move the 4,820 schools within 96 school districts in the province. At the center of the improvement strategy was a simple question that we have expanded upon in this chapter: "How we can further improve teaching and learning so that all students demonstrate equal levels of success in applying key cognitive skills to complete rigorous and complex learning tasks?" We can break down the key ingredients of exceptional teaching and learning into six parts so that all school sites can develop precision of pedagogy.

1. Clearly define the barriers to student learning that are preventing all students from successfully completing rigorous and complex learning tasks.

2. Identify the key cognitive skills that if students develop mastery will result in significant growth in student learning.

3. Clarify which high-yield instructional practices will have the greatest impact on improving student acquisition of these key cognitive skills.

4. Determine the evidence of learning that will best inform the impact of teaching on student learning.

5. Make common agreements as to how teaching and learning will be approached to test this theory of action and make adjustments based on the impact on student learning.

6. Collectively commit to learning together how best to maximize the impact of teaching on student learning.

Taking Action

John Hattie has become the primary source of research for maximizing the impact on student learning in his publication of *Visible Learning* and subsequently *Visible Learning for Teachers*, which ranked the effect sizes of instructional strategies. In 2016 the rankings were updated to include a new number-one influence on student learning: collective teacher efficacy. The greatest impact on student learning occurs when school staff have a shared belief in their collective ability to positively influence student learning. Marzano (2007) has framed the challenge of developing the capacity and confidence of a school staff through his seminal research in *The Art and Science of Teaching*:

> The best that research can do is tell us which strategies have a good chance (i.e., high probability) of working well with students. Classroom teachers must determine which strategies to employ with the right students at the right time. In effect, a good part of effective teaching is an art, hence the title, *The Art and Science of Teaching*.

Clearly there is an art and science to developing collective expertise among the staff of a school site. To see this in action we can look toward another performance-based learning activity that requires instructional coherence, collaborative inquiry, and precision of practice: gymnastics. If you have ever had the opportunity to observe a gymnastics practice in action, you would understand. In a large room would be about four groups of gymnasts ranging from beginners to those with exceptional abilities. But what would be seen are similar routines being practiced by each group with increasing difficulty and precision as gymnasts ascend to the next group. There is a progression for developing, acquiring, and perfecting each highly structured skill before moving into the next group, where more complexity is added and a precision of practice is expected. You can actually see all four groups practicing at the same time and make explicit connections to the routines being learned that lead to developing the technical skills and artistic ability of an exceptional gymnast. And the trainers of these gymnasts transition from leading beginners in highly structured activities to ultimately serving as coaches who pinpoint subtle nuances of extremely difficult performances that define who will win the national championship. This is the mindset and process that school leaders and teachers need to adopt to develop collective expertise among the school staff. Some teachers or teams are beginners that need more explicit and structured support, others need more coaching and feedback, and some want specific insights on subtle shifts in instruction that make the difference in learning for certain students.

An effective approach to the process of developing collective expertise that allows for this gradual release of deeper levels of ownership and ability to improve student learning is through the use of a series of protocols (Figure 4.3). The sequence of this series of protocols is similar to what was shared in the example of the gymnasts with a structure and process that is designed to create instructional coherence, foster collaborative inquiry, and develop precision of pedagogy. What follows (Figures 4.4–4.10) is the sequence of protocols that Jay and the team at InnovateEd have used with schools and districts. The protocols are a beginning point that provide structure and support, then transition to adaptations and improvements by school staff to make the work their own, and finally result in a staff having the collective efficacy to carry on the work with high levels of confidence without the need of protocols to guide the work at hand.

Figure 4.3   School Site Protocol Cycle

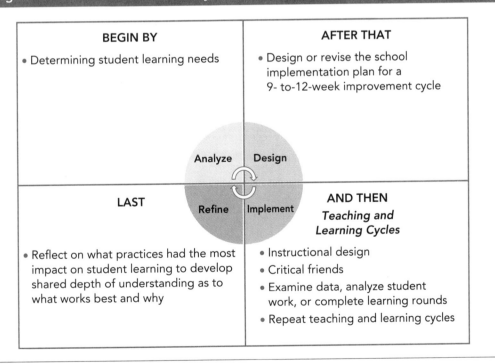

BEGIN BY	AFTER THAT
• Determining student learning needs	• Design or revise the school implementation plan for a 9- to-12-week improvement cycle

Analyze | Design
Refine | Implement

LAST	AND THEN *Teaching and Learning Cycles*
• Reflect on what practices had the most impact on student learning to develop shared depth of understanding as to what works best and why	• Instructional design • Critical friends • Examine data, analyze student work, or complete learning rounds • Repeat teaching and learning cycles

© 2022 InnovateEd

Figure 4.4   Determining Student Learning Needs

Purpose: A process protocol for teams to strategically design a tool for monitoring impact using data analysis. It is designed to be used after teams have determined what a years' worth of progress will look like for each student and before they engage in instructional design work.

Opening 5 minutes	Review norms. Facilitator explains or reviews the purpose and process of the protocol. Group reviews school implementation plan and makes connections to the cycle of inquiry.
Calibrating Criteria for Student Baseline Status 30–45 minutes	Participants calibrate criteria for students' current level of proficiency as it relates to multiple measures of student learning and performance, previously identified when the team determined what a year's worth of progress would look like and how they would measure a year's worth of progress. • What level of performance will we use to indicate that students are achieving above, at, near, or below the level of proficiency for our agreed-upon measures?
Record, Identify, Sort, and Post 45–90 minutes (depending on number of students)	Participants document each student's baseline data based on the criteria the team determined. • Document each student by name and/or grade level/class period and record their current level of performance. • Document each student's growth target based on team decision for measuring at least 1 year of growth. • Identify each student's current performance level based on calibrated criteria for current level of proficiency. • Sort all students by class period, then by proficiency level, then by performance level as needed based on criteria and team agreements. • Create a visual representation for the team to examine simultaneously.
Determining Student Subgroups 30–45 minutes (depending on number of students)	Participants determine and list significant subgroups. • Which subgroups do we need to be aware of when designing a response to this data (i.e., students with disabilities, English learners, etc.)?
Identify, Document, and Sort 30–45 minutes (depending on number of students)	Participants identify students by subgroup needs. • Participants sort students within performance categories by subgroup needs. • Create a visual representation for individuals and the team to examine.

Group Discussion and Next Step Commitments 45–60 minutes	Participants discuss implications of students' baseline data and growth targets. <ul><li>Ask questions.</li><li>Reflect upon reality of students' current levels of performance</li><li>Make connections to the school implementation plan</li><li>Discuss implications for instructional design based on current reality and school implementation plan</li></ul> Team members make and commit to next steps.
Debrief 10 minutes	Team discusses what worked and didn't work with the process and the protocols. Group reflects on the norms.

© 2022 InnovateEd

Figure 4.5 Designing and Revising the School Implementation Plan	
Purpose: A process protocol for SLTs to determine the progress of implementation, lead indicators, and lead measures to refine the school implementation plan.	
Opening 5 minutes	Review norms, assign roles, and reinforce purpose and process of the protocol.
Dialogue Around Successes and Progress 30–60 minutes	Team members dialogue around individual and collective successes in implementing the plan and/or leading the work. <ul><li>What commitments did the team follow through on?</li><li>What aspects of the plan was the team able to implement?</li><li>What evidence has been collected to indicate success or progress made?</li></ul>
Dialogue Around Challenges and Obstacles 30–60 minutes	Team members dialogue around individual and collective challenges with implementing the plan and/or leading the work. <ul><li>What if any commitments did the team not stick to? What got in the way?</li><li>What aspects of the plan was the team not able to implement? Why?</li><li>What evidence has been collected to indicate challenges or obstacles?</li></ul>
Refine the School Implementation Plan 150–180 minutes	<ul><li>NOTE: Rather than deleting or replacing words, phrases, and so on, many teams prefer to keep a running log of their journey by color-coding revisions, dating revisions, or saving a new copy of their plan.</li><li>Team members dialogue, discuss, and make decisions about the school implementation plan</li></ul>

(Continued)

Figure 4.5	(Continued)
	Considerations • Focus and Outcome: Does your focus need narrowing or refining? Is this the right focus area given the needs of your students? Has evidence been collected that suggests a foundational or underlying issue? Is the outcome a clear, measurable target to aim toward? • Student Success Indicators: What are your success indicators? Does your staff believe these student skills and behaviors will lead to achieving the focus and outcome? Are they lead indicators (predictive and influenceable)? • Staff Practices: What staff practices do we need to implement or refine for students to gain the skills and demonstrate the behaviors outlined as student success indicators? Are these staff practices embraced? Will all or most of the staff commit to implementing them? • School Supports: Have you outlined the supports staff members need to implement staff practices outlined in your plan? Are there specific supports and/or resources that are needed from the district? • Evidence of Learning: Are these lead measures? Do they assess the students' abilities to demonstrate one or more success indicators? Does the staff believe these are valid and reliable measures? To what extent is the staff calibrated around these measures? • Timeline: Is the timeline reasonable? Is it a specific date or window of time? Will your timeline increase or decrease commitment and internal accountability to the plan?
Clarify Next Steps and Solidify Commitments 20–30 minutes	Team members discuss next steps and make commitments to one another. • How will you re-engage staff with a refined school implementation plan? • How will you restore or improve commitment? • What evidence of learning will you bring back to the next session?
Debrief 10 minutes	Group discusses what worked and didn't work with the process and the protocol. Facilitator asks the group to reflect on the norms.

© 2022 InnovateEd

Figure 4.6	**Collaborative Instructional Design**
Purpose: A process for strategically designing lessons and tasks related to the standards and based on the school-wide focus area.	
Opening 5 minutes	Review norms. Participants review the focus, purpose, and process of the protocol.
Design the Learning Target 10 minutes	Design the learning target based on the following: • Selection of state standards • Determination of Depth of Knowledge (DOK, rigor and complexity) level *What is the explicit expectation for mastery of standards-based skills and concepts?* *What is the explicit expectation for level of cognitive application (DOK level)?*
Define the Performance Outcome 10 minutes	Define student performance outcomes based on the following: • Concepts and skills students must apply • Level of cognitive application • Student product or performance • Feedback to the student *How do your rubrics, exemplars, or models clarify expected student performance?* *Is there a clear connection between student performance and mastery of standards-based skills? Do the prompts and questions align with the expected level of cognitive application?*
Develop a Sequence of Learning Tasks for Each Phase of the Instruction 45 minutes	Develop opportunities for student learning that provide the following: • Connect to prior knowledge and build background knowledge • Promote development of literacy and critical thinking skills • Develop student metacognition • Support student collaboration and dialog • Provide feedback to students as part of the learning process **Student Task, Guiding Questions, and Formative Feedback** *How does the task guide student mastery of skills and concepts and cognitive application?* *What questions engage students in deliberate practice of skills and concepts with scaffolding to support cognitive application?* *How do the students actively engage in formative feedback to assess progress toward mastery of skills and concepts and expected level of cognitive application?*

(Continued)

Figure 4.6   (Continued)

	Literacy Strategies and Engagement Strategies *What are the student supports for close reading, evidence-based arguments, academic language, structured collaboration, and evidence-based writing?* **Targeted Student Support** *How are student group structures, questions, supports, and formative feedback differentiated based on levels of skill and concept mastery, cognitive application, active engagement, and social-emotional and behavioral needs? What specific support is provided to English learners, students with disabilities, and other targeted student groups?*
We Agree 5 minutes	Identify and discuss one to three specific strategies each team member commits to implement.
Debrief 5 minutes	What did you gain as a team from the process? Discuss next steps and set date to discuss impact of instructional on student learning. Team reflects on norms

© 2022 InnovateEd

Figure 4.7   Critical Friends Protocol

Purpose: A process protocol that allows individuals or groups to reflect upon inherent assumptions, clarity, and proposed outcomes with a professional peer group.	
Opening 5 minutes	Review norms. Facilitator explains or reviews the purpose and process of the protocol.
Presentation of Experience, Strategy, Student Work, Lesson, and so on. 5 minutes (one person at a time)	NOTE: During this stage of the protocol, one participant or team is sharing without interruption. The remaining members of the team or group should listen attentively and avoid interrupting the presenter. Participant describes the strategy, experience, student work samples, lesson, and so on. They should also share specific challenges or wonderings for the team to provide input on during the critical friends portion of the protocol. After the participant describes what they brought to the session, they should pass around evidence and artifacts for others to briefly preview.
Briefly Preview Work and/or Lesson and Ask Clarifying Questions 5 minutes	Allow participants a short time to preview the evidence, artifacts, and so on. Participants can ask clarifying questions about the information being shared.

Critical Friends 10 minutes	The presenter should be prepared to record thoughts while the group discusses the lesson and student work (they should avoid speaking during this portion of the protocol). NOTE: Facilitator reminds participants that all comments should be evidence-based and support the area(s) that the presenter asked for feedback around and/or areas that support the school focus. Plus Round: Participants should each take turns stating something positive about the presenter's material. Participants should use the phrase, "I saw, I observed, or I noticed . . . because . . ." citing specific evidence. Delta Round: Participants should each take turns stating something they wonder about. A wondering should address a question, concern, or possible extension or improvement of the work. Participants should use the phrase, "I wonder . . ." Share Round: Participants share any additional ideas or resources to support the presenter. Participants should use the language, "Something to consider for next time might be . . ."
Reflection 5–10 minutes	The presenter reflects on the insights provided during the critical friends' stage of the protocol and may respond to wonderings from the group or ask further questions for support. NOTE: Repeat rows two through five for each presenter.
Debrief 5 minutes	Participants discuss what worked and didn't work with the process and the protocol. Facilitator asks the group to reflect on the norms.

© 2022 InnovateEd

Figure 4.8   Examining Data

Purpose: A deductive process to guide groups through analysis of quantitative data to identify strengths and problems of practice.	
Opening 5 minutes	Review norms. Assign roles (facilitator, recorder, and timekeeper). Explain and review the purpose and process of the protocol. Facilitator briefly describes the data to be discussed. Participants ask clarifying questions about the process, data, and so on.
Gathering Facts 10 minutes	Individuals silently observe the data and list facts. • What parts of this data catch your attention? Just the facts. Group discusses observations made.

(Continued)

Figure 4.8	**(Continued)**
Making Evidence-Based Inferences 10 minutes	Individuals silently make inferences about the data. Facilitator encourages participants to support statements with evidence from the data. • What does the data tell us? • What does the data not tell us? Group discusses inferences made and comes to consensus.
Identify Strengths 5 minutes	Facilitator asks the group to look for indications of success in the data. • What good news is there to celebrate? Group discusses strengths.
Identify Problems of Practice 10 minutes	Individuals silently identify potential problems of practice. • What are the problems of practice suggested by the data? Facilitator helps group narrow problems of practice to one to two areas of priority.
Brainstorm Next Steps 5 minutes	Facilitator reminds group to think outside of the box. • What could we do differently to improve results? • What ideas do you have for addressing the problem of practice? Individuals silently brainstorm ideas for acting on one or two problems of practice.
Determine Next Steps 10 minutes	Individuals share their ideas for addressing problems of practice. Facilitator helps group narrow ideas. Group determines how they will address problems of practice.
Design Next Steps 10 minutes	Group designs an action plan. • What will you commit to doing differently? • How will you do it? • How will you gather evidence? • What support do you need? • When will you reconvene to examine the evidence? • How and when will you share relevant findings with other stakeholders?
Debrief 5 minutes	All participants discuss what worked and didn't work with the protocol. Facilitator asks the group to reflect on the norms.

© 2022 InnovateEd

Figure 4.9 Analyzing Student Work

Purpose: A process to guide the analysis of student work, resulting in individual next steps and team commitments.	
Opening 5 minutes	Review norms. Review focus for the meeting. Reinforce purpose and process of the protocol.
Calibration (as appropriate)	If the student work to be analyzed is rubric-based, then review of the rubric and calibration is done at this point.
Presentation of Work and Clarifying Questions 15 minutes per participant	Teacher describes the student work and lesson that was conducted, including the learning target related to the area of focus. Place each set of student work samples in its own stack at the center of the table (should have multiple stacks depending on number of different work samples). Participants can take time to ask clarifying questions about the student work, lesson(s), or the protocol itself. Repeat calibration, presentation of work, and clarifying questions for each presenter.
Review Student Work 30 minutes	Allow participants sufficient time to view student work samples from each stack. Participants should note how the student work demonstrates the area of focus. Record strengths and areas for growth. After reviewing student work, participants should record their reflections and recommendations related to the school focus area.
Group Discussion and Group Commitments 5–10 minutes	Participants discuss their reflections and recommendations based on the student work and implications for next steps. Presenter documents individual commitments.
Team Reflection and Commitments 10–15 minutes	Group reflects on successes and challenges. • Are there patterns or trends in the student work products across multiple classrooms, grade levels, and/or content areas? Discuss impact on school implementation plan and how to disseminate the analysis and next steps with the principal, school leadership team, and teacher teams. Team discusses and documents commitments.
Debrief 5 minutes	Team members discuss what worked and didn't work with the protocol. Participants reflect on norms.

© 2022 InnovateEd

Figure 4.10	Learning Rounds

Purpose: Provides an authentic experience for groups to gather information about students' skills, behaviors, and dispositions relevant to the site focus area while simultaneously calibrating understanding of student tasks. Participants have an opportunity to reflect on the experience and determine individual, team, and group next steps.

Opening and Pre-Brief: Clarify and Discuss Purpose, Focus Area(s), and Norms
 	
30–45 minutes
	District and site administrators or teacher leader(s) facilitate conversation around purpose, focus area(s), and norms:
	
	• Facilitator reviews district and site academic priorities through a brief, informative, interactive dialog.
	
	• Facilitator explains or reminds the team of the purpose of learning rounds and previews the protocol, reflection tools, and notetaking templates.
	
	• Team reviews focus for the meeting—connecting back to the school implementation plan.
	
	• Facilitator explains importance of essential professional norms:
	
	   ○ Focus on the students.
	
	   ○ Be engaged in the observation, reflection, and discussion.
	
	   ○ Be respectful of the students and the teachers in classrooms.
	
	   ○ Hold strict confidentiality—only trends and patterns of student learning and next steps for student learning will be discussed outside of the learning rounds; specifics with regard to individual classrooms will not be discussed outside of learning rounds.
	
	   ○ Refrain from making evaluative comments.
	
	• Team establishes procedural norms such as entering and exiting, taking notes, or talking to one another inside classrooms, talking to students in the classrooms, and so on.

Learning Rounds Approx. 10–20 minutes in each classroom with 5 minute debriefs between classrooms	Classroom Visits: • Participants will observe students using the documents in the Learning Rounds Guide for reference while following agreed-upon norms. • Team will gather in a standing circle away from the classroom to share evidence that was observed (i.e., student skills, behaviors, structures, etc. as outlined in the Learning Rounds Guide). • Facilitator and team members will adhere to professional norms and agreed-upon procedural norms to ask probing questions and guide conversations. • Everyone in the team will be given the chance to share observations as they pertain to visible evidence of student learning, but participants may choose to pass. • Team members will calibrate observations and agree upon the evidence observed.

Debrief 45–60 minutes	Final Debrief—Using Student-Centered Statements: • Team members will calibrate and agree upon the evidence of student skills and behaviors observed. • Group members will discuss next steps for students. What opportunities, practices, and/or supports do your students need to go from x to x+1? • Facilitator will chart reflections to be shared later at staff, leadership, and/or team meetings. • Participants will discuss how the evidence gathered and next steps for student learning might inform school-wide efforts. • Team will decide how they can relay the information gathered to the principal, SLT, and/or other teams. • Team members discuss what worked and didn't work with the learning rounds protocol.

© 2022 InnovateEd

Guiding Continuous Improvement 5

The concept of continuous improvement has always been a central focus in education whether framed as outcome-based, process-oriented, or culturally driven. Student equity would be an outcome-based model of continuous improvement wherein achieving equitable outcomes for all students is the key driver of improvement efforts. A collaborative inquiry cycle that guides individuals and teams in the process of continuously improving practices and student learning results is foundational for achieving equitable growth in student learning. A culture of continuous improvement establishes a common vision, shared purpose and agreed-upon structures, and processes and practices for sustaining improvement efforts. These three concepts of continuous improvement are not mutually exclusive but rather are interdependent of each other, meaning that all three must be in place for a school district or site to enact and sustain the continuous improvement of practices and growth in student learning.

It is rare to see all three concepts in action, and this is what separates those schools and districts that sustain improvement efforts versus those with short bursts of improvement that are not sustainable. In reality, continuous improvement is a common phrase that does not always have clarity of action for moving the work forward. There is a continuum of sorts for taking action because it is easy to establish outcomes for student learning, more difficult to develop agreed-upon processes that guide improvement efforts, and challenging to create a culture of continuous improvement because this calls upon leaders at all levels to reinforce a common vision, shared purpose, and agreed-upon processes and practices. It is not surprising then that most school districts and sites have defined outcomes for student learning, some have established agreed-upon improvement processes, and few have cultivated a culture of continuous improvement.

> A culture of continuous improvement establishes a common vision, shared purpose and agreed-upon structures, processes and practices for sustaining improvement efforts.

An approach that simplifies the complexity of guiding continuous improvement is to structure these three interdependent concepts into what, how, and why questions. What are the equitable outcomes for learning that have been established for all students? How can teachers and leaders engage in an agreed-upon improvement process to achieve equitable growth in student learning? Is a culture of continuous improvement valued by all members of the organization? If so, then have all staff embraced a common vision, shared purpose, and agreed-upon processes and practices that ensure sustainability of improvement efforts? These four questions can serve as a litmus test as to the potential for a school district or site to effectively guide continuous improvement. Those that dedicate the time, energy, and support needed to respond to these questions with depth and specificity will reap the rewards of sustaining equitable growth in student learning.

Another critical success factor for consideration is what could be called "optimal timeframes" for continuous improvement cycles. These timeframes vary at the district, school, and classroom levels to promote a structured process of support, monitoring, and feedback. In *Districts on the Move* we had advocated for 3-week improvement cycles at the teacher team level, 6-week cycles at the school level, and 9-week cycles at the district level. This would play out as teams of teachers completed two 3-week improvement cycles leading up to a school-wide sharing of progress and impact at the end of this 6-week period. At this time, the school leadership team would learn of the progress, impact, and next steps of each teacher team in an effort to understand how best to move forward the continuous improvement of teaching and learning. District leaders and school principals would review progress, impact, and needs of every school site at the 9-week period so that there was clarity as to how best to support the improvement efforts of every school site. This also serves as an opportunity to share promising practices, identify common problems of practices, and revise both district-level and school site action plans for improving teaching and learning. The purpose of these nested cycles of inquiry is to reduce variance in student learning growth within and among school sites by focusing improvement efforts on the most impactful teaching and learning practices and overcoming common problems of practice.

Problems of Practice and Promising Practices

One of the most challenging endeavors for school districts and sites is establishing evidence-based cycles of inquiry that guide the continuous improvement of leadership, teaching, and learning. There are three primary reasons for the challenge. First is that continuous improvement is a concept that is not deeply understood by educators at large. As we have noted, there must be a common focus for achieving equitable student outcomes, a clearly delineated process that guides improvement efforts, and a culture that embraces a common vision, shared purpose, and agreed-upon processes and practices. Second is that continuous improvement cannot be the responsibility of teachers, principals, or district leaders, rather it is a collective responsibility wherein each level guides their own improvement efforts and intentionally supports the continuous improvement of all schools within the district. Last is that evidence of impact on student learning growth must inform the continuous improvement of practices and be used as a means for identifying promising practices and clarifying problems of practice.

The issue at hand for many school districts and sites is that guiding continuous improvement has not yet been described in the depth and specificity needed to guide recurring improvement cycles that inform progress and impact at the classroom, school, and district levels. For many school districts, continuous improvement is the responsibility of school sites. And similarly, for many school sites the responsibility for continuous improvement falls upon teacher teams. These cultural norms create disconnects among district leaders, principals, and teachers as to the roles and responsibilities for co-leading improvement cycles. This lack of clarity is a barrier to collectively defining improvement processes that guide the work at the district, school, and classroom levels. And ultimately, these cultural and structural issues prevent school sites and districts from achieving equitable growth in student learning. One could say that it is a vicious cycle that needs some form of intervention to move forward with more clarity and internal accountability. However, continuous improvement cannot be prescribed or directed, rather it takes conjoint action and collective responsibility.

Of all the school districts with whom InnovateEd has partnered with over the past 14 years, one stands out in having effectively guided continuous improvement at all levels: Rosedale Union Elementary District. This work occurred over a 3-year period of time under the leadership of Superintendent John Mendiburu and Assistant Superintendent Sue Lemon. Improvement efforts at Rosedale centered on co-leading cycles of inquiry among the district team, principal collaboratives, school leadership teams, and site teacher teams. School sites were organized into triads with district staff liaisons who served as cohort learning partners. School leadership teams and principal collaboratives were structured to engage in collaborative inquiry of student learning evidence for continuous improvement of practices and student learning results. Initially, improvement efforts focused on developing capacity of school leadership teams to guide 6-week evidenced-based cycles of inquiry. As capacity improved, the efforts then shifted to supporting teacher leaders with facilitating teacher team collaborative inquiry in 3- to 4-week instructional cycles. The next step was to create feedback loops connecting evidence of learning from teacher teams and the improvement efforts of school leadership teams so that principals and district leaders could adapt and adjust support systems based on the needs of each school site. The driving force was knowing the collective impact at the classroom, school, and district levels as part of recurring improvement cycles focused on evidence of student learning. Rosedale adopted the slogan "Know Your Impact" to acknowledge that each person in the district makes a difference for all students' learning and long-term growth. This was strategic in that team structures for collaborative inquiry needed to be driven by evidence of learning from student work produced in classrooms to more clearly inform the impact of instructional supports across all school sites.

> The fundamental purpose of all teams is to move forward a common agenda of achieving equitable outcomes for all students through an agreed upon improvement process that focuses on evidence of impact on student learning growth.

In Long Beach Unified School District under the leadership of Chris and his team, a similar process played out at a much larger scale; Rosedale has nine schools whereas Long Beach has 84. Scaling of continuous improvement cycles, although more complex, has the same foundational aspects of clearly defined equitable student outcomes, agreed-upon improvement processes, and a culture of continuous improvement that engages all levels of the district in seeking evidence of impact to identify promising practices and clarify problems of practice. Essential team structures are inclusive of a district team that serves as liaisons to school clusters, each with a principal collaborative and school leadership teams that support site-based teacher teams. The integrated improvement cycles at the district, school, and classroom levels help ensure that all schools are progressing toward achieving equitable growth in student learning. As noted by Mary Jean Gallagher, with whom Jay has had the pleasure of leading this work over many years, these team structures are not a hierarchy but rather a huddle, meaning that the fundamental purpose of all teams is to move forward a common agenda of achieving equitable outcomes for all students through an agreed-upon improvement process that focuses on evidence of impact on student learning growth. This ensures that all schools have clarity of focus with systems of support for engaging in the continuous improvement of teaching and learning.

District and School Story

After the last school site visits, Assistant Superintendent Erin MacFarland and Principal Jacob Westfall had come to the conclusion that a final step of their action research would be to better understand how school sites utilize evidence to guide improvement efforts. A common practice of Anywhere School District was to provide principals with data reports generated by the central office. Jacob, as principal of Somewhere School, was accustomed to receiving and reviewing these reports with his fellow principals and district staff at periodic principal meetings. However, he and Erin were not clear as to how each principal then used these reports with school staff.

After having reviewed the data as a group at the principal meeting, Erin explained that she was interested in better understanding how these data were used among schools. She structured small group conversations so that principals could share their site processes and practices and then asked each group to share their insights. As might have been expected, the responses varied, but the overall consensus was that principals provided school staff with a copy of the data report, reviewed highlights of the data at a staff meeting, and asked staff to create action steps in response to the data. Erin thanked the principals for sharing how the data reports were utilized among school sites and then asked if the generation and sharing of data by the central office were helpful. Most principals expressed appreciation because these reports reduced the burden among school sites. Erin agreed to continue to provide the reports but asked that a more common process be adopted among schools for using the data to guide the improvement of practices and student learning results. She asked that each principal provide her with a more detailed description of their school site's data-driven improvement processes and explained that she would be following up with some school sites for a visit to see how this work played out in action.

Jacob knew that Erin was setting the stage for the final school site visits. After the principal meeting, he suggested to Erin that these next visits could be structured to either observe a school leadership team meeting or be during weekly teacher

(Continued)

(Continued)

collaboration time. Erin suggested that they do both and could meet with the leadership team for 30 minutes prior to the start of Wednesday morning collaboration time. In this way they could learn from teacher leaders how the school uses data to inform practices as well as gain insights from seeing teacher teams in action. Jacob liked this combination of a focus group meeting paired with an observation of teacher collaboration and thought this could be a great way to calibrate processes and practices within each school and across school sites. Erin agreed that calibrating processes and practices would be powerful but recognized that there were not common agreements as to the role of principals, school leadership teams, or teacher teams in how data were used to guide and inform improvement efforts. So rather than creating guiding questions for the upcoming visits, Jacob and Erin agreed to come up with their own set of processes and practices from which to calibrate school site visits. The combined version was finalized as a calibration tool that would guide the dialog and observations during school site visits.

Scheduling of school site visits had required Erin to be more directly involved with principals than Jacob this time because she had announced the upcoming visits at the last principal meeting. Several principals who had not been visited in the past offered to host a visitation. Erin wanted to maintain the same four schools for the visitation schedule so had decided it was best to invite all principals to attend the site visits as a co-learning opportunity. The hope was that the observations would allow for additional dialog among principals at the conclusion of each site visit and provide an opportunity for them to share insights about their own schools. Erin was happy to see that all principals had signed up to attend one of the four site visits, which would allow her to capture key learnings from all schools. Jacob would be attending each school visit but was fine with this because he was usually perceived among his colleagues as being eager to learn.

Jacob was a little anxious the Wednesday morning of the first school site visit. He was always in attendance at his teacher collaboration meetings and arrived a little late to the focus group meeting because he wanted to be sure his school would be running smoothly in his absence. Upon entering the room, he took a seat next to a few other principals who were listening to members of the school leadership team describe how they used data at their school site. On the whiteboard he saw written "school-wide processes and practices," and underneath were some key insights written by Erin, who was facilitating the focus group meeting. Upon reading these more closely, Jacob realized that the bullets were identical to what had been shared at the principal meeting: analyze data reports, discuss data at the staff meeting, and create action steps in response to the data. Not wanting to offend the principal of the school, Jacob apologized for being late and then asked how the school leadership team used data to guide the work of the school site. The principal was quick to respond first and generally reiterated the three bullets on the whiteboard. Jacob thanked the principal for the information and then inquired how teacher teams use data during collaboration time. The principal stated that that is when action steps are created based on the data in the reports.

Erin had not considered that other principals would also ask questions of the host school, but when a visiting principal asked if he could ask a question, she nervously obliged. The principal asked, "Do you review data only when these reports are shared, or do you also analyze other forms of data at your school site?" There was a long moment of silence, and then one teacher spoke to share that her team indeed did look at other types of data as a team but was not certain if other teams did as well. This prompted another visiting principal to ask, "What data do your school find to be most valuable or informative?" Again there was another long moment of silence until one of the most senior teachers shared that the data reports were not that informative because she did not value the district assessments as much as her own classroom assessments. Erin, in hearing this, asked the teacher to share more so she could write a clear statement on the whiteboard. The teacher was hesitant but then shared that the district assessments did not always align with what had been taught so the data were not informative.

Jacob could tell that the school principal was uncomfortable with the conversation and so expressed appreciation for the comments from both teachers. He then made a statement and asked if the

(Continued)

(Continued)

teachers agreed with his comment, "So would it be fair to say that the reason you review these data reports is to comply with what could be considered as a district expectation?" A teacher among the group had smiled and nodded in agreement, and Jacob asked her if she agreed with his statement. After briefing looking at the school principal, the teacher stated that this was the case and that her team did not find much value in reviewing the data and creating action steps. Erin did not want these meetings to be seen negatively among the school leadership team, and so she thanked them all for their insights and shared that what was learned would be used to improve how the district supports school sites.

Following the focus group meeting, Erin, Jacob, and the other visiting principals were invited to join any of the teacher teams during collaboration time. Erin and Jacob decided to visit the teams together, and the other principals formed their own group. Each had time to sit in on two teacher collaboration meetings and capture insights. At the conclusion of collaboration time, all of the principals and Erin met in the site principal's conference room to debrief. Because this was the first time that principals had visited each other's schools during collaboration time, Erin wanted to set some norms for the group, asking that all refrain from personal comments and only discuss what was seen occurring during collaboration time. The site principal expressed a desire to hear from the group and appeared open to their insights and feedback.

Jacob broke the ice and noted that all teacher teams had the data reports and were discussing trends and patterns. A principal from the other group reinforced this observation and noted that one team seemed to be more comfortable with the data analysis process. This prompted Erin to ask if there was an agreed-upon process or protocol at the school that guided teacher teams in the analysis of data. The site principal shared that teachers understood that each team was to create a few action steps in response to the data. Another principal commented that an agreed-upon process would be helpful at his school site. All principals seemed to agree that not all teacher teams at their sites had the same level of ability with analyzing data and creating clear and impactful action steps. Erin suggested that she could coordinate a few district meetings with school site representatives to create a draft process for data analysis that would inform instructional responses.

Before concluding their debriefing, Jacob leaned over to Erin and asked how they were going to complete the calibration tool that had been created for the site visits. She shrugged her shoulders with uncertainty; the new format would not provide an opportunity for them to chart key insights because Jacob had to return to his school. Jacob suggested that they share the tool with the principals in attendance for their own reflections. Erin agreed, and so she introduced the tool as a reflection process for site principals and asked that they each complete the chart on their own time and then discuss their thoughts at the next principal meeting. One principal asked whether this tool was the new expectation from the district office for school sites. Another asked a few clarifying questions. Erin reinforced that this was only a tool and that it could be refined to become district guidance if school principals wanted to do so. Most were in agreement that having a common tool to calibrate school site processes and practices would be advantageous if there was a way that it could be finalized with input from school principals and staff. The departing agreement was that each principal would use the tool for their own reflection and share the tool with school staff to gather feedback for improvement and refinement. As Jacob and Erin walked across the parking lot toward their cars, each had a sense of relief on their faces because this visitation process was new for the schools and principals. As Erin stepped into her car, she said to Jacob, "I think this visitation process has a lot of potential, and I can see us doing this on a regular basis." Jacob smiled in agreement.

Erin's feeling of enlightenment quickly faded when she received a phone call from the principal who was hosting the next school visit. To prepare for the visit, the principal had shared the calibration tool with school staff, and as a result, a few members of the school leadership team were upset. The visit was scheduled to begin in an hour, and Erin wanted to quickly understand the problem. The principal shared that the issue was with the calibration tool in that some teachers felt that they were being

(Continued)

(Continued)

told what to do and how to do it. Erin recalled that at the school visitation last week, principals had agreed to share the tool with staff for input and feedback. She asked the principal if this was understood by the school staff. From the way the principal was describing the problem, Erin could tell that the frustration was emanating from resistance to change among the school staff. And the principal was as resistant as the staff to any changes of school processes or practices.

As Jacob arrived in the parking lot of the school, Erin pulled him aside and gave him an update on the situation. He was not surprised and suggested that Erin be the charter and he the facilitator because this could help diffuse any issues that may come up with the school leadership team. A few other principals were already waiting in the office, and then all were led as a group to the meeting room. Erin explained the purpose of the visit and then moved to the whiteboard. As planned, she asked that Jacob facilitate so that she could chart the insights from the teachers and site principal. Before he could begin, one of the teachers held up a copy of the calibration tool and smugly asked if this was a new district expectation for school sites. Jacob was quick to respond and simply stated, "No it's not a district expectation, but what are your thoughts and reactions to the tool? Your feedback is important." The teacher shared that the tool seemed prescriptive and unnecessary. One of the visiting principals suggested that the calibration tool not be the focus of conversation, but instead they would like to learn how the school used data to inform practices.

There was a feeling of resistance in the room on the part of the leadership team and site principal to respond. So another visiting principal referenced the data report from the central office and asked how the staff used the report for decision-making. A teacher from the site seemed confused, so Jacob asked him if he had a question. The teacher's response was that he had never seen this report before but did recognize some of the data points that had been presented at a staff meeting. Erin then reminded the group that she was charting insights from the school and asked the leadership team what she should write about the use of data at the school. The site principal then stood and shared that the data reports were shared at staff meetings as part of an update of school progress. Jacob, in an effort to assist Erin with charting, asked the group if they agreed with his statement, "So what I understand is that the data report becomes part of quarterly staff meeting presentations, but teachers do not receive a copy of the report for discussion in their teams for creating action steps." The majority of the leadership team members nodded in agreement, and one teacher added that teachers use their own data to make decisions about how to support student learning.

A visiting principal then inquired as to how staff decided what type of data was best for making these decisions. Erin, not wanting to upset the teachers in the room, said that she valued their input and wanted to chart their ideas. The leadership team members seemed to appreciate Erin's comment, and so several shared the varying types of data that each team used during collaboration time. It was clear that there was not a consistent process nor any agreed-upon data points that guided the work of teachers in the school. Jacob thought that this lack of consistency must be the source of frustration with the calibration tool: resistance to change. He then returned to his role as facilitator and reminded the group of the time, noting that collaboration time would begin soon. He thanked the teachers and site principal for their participation and insights.

Rather than leaving the room to visit teacher teams, one of the visiting principals suggested that the administrators stay in the room to debrief. Erin asked for clarification as to the purpose of staying to debrief, and the principal's answer was surprising to her: "I would like to discuss with this group the elephant in the room. The data reports don't appear to be valuable for school sites, but there doesn't seem to be any consistency as to how data is being used to inform teaching and learning. This could be the same problem for all schools, and I'd like to hear ideas from others as to how we can fix this issue." Jacob asked if the calibration tool would be helpful with this dialog, and all agreed that it was a good starting point. So the group spent the remainder of the time discussing the calibration tool to better understand the intent and make connections as to how data-driven inquiry processes could become more effective

(Continued)

(Continued)

and consistent among school sites. At the conclusion of the debriefing, Erin thanked the site principal and visiting principals for the productive conversation and then asked an awkward question, "Why is it that the dialog we have at principal meetings is not as frank and robust as this meeting?" The site principal, showing a sign of less resistance, stated that this conversation was about the work and occurred at a school site, but principal meetings seemed to be too structured and removed from the work. Erin then suggested that in the future these site-based meetings could occur along with principal meetings so that there was a way to dive deeper into the work. There appeared to be agreement among all principals that this would be valuable and worth their time.

Having had participated in a previous school site visit, the principal of the school perceived to be fragmented thought it best to call Jacob and discuss the structure of the upcoming site visit. Jacob thanked the principal for reaching out to him and asked whether there was concern among the school staff about the site visit. There was not, but the principal did share that the staff were difficult to lead and that there was uncertainty as to how they would react to multiple school principals asking pointed questions about the use of data. Jacob suggested that it may be better to structure the visit as more of a co-learning opportunity and asked whether the principal would prefer the staff share current practices or have more of an open dialog among all participants. The latter was preferred, and so Jacob informed Erin of the change in plans. At first Erin was frustrated with the change but then thought that it might be good to have a less structured dialog as was suggested in the debriefing at the last school visit.

What was initially planned as a focus group meeting had now become an open dialog about how school sites use data to inform teaching and learning. Rather than charting key insights, Erin positioned herself within the circle of chairs and framed the purpose of the meeting as a conversation about the use of data at school sites. She also mentioned the data reports and the calibration tool as reference points to start the conversations with teachers and principals in the room. The site principal spoke first, feeling a sense of obligation for causing the change in meeting structure. The principal commented that the past three visitations at the site had had an impact on the school staff, and there was recognition of the need and desire to work together more effectively. Erin expressed appreciation for the comments and thought that being vulnerable herself was important in stating, "I want all of you to know that no one at the central office believes they have the answer for how best to support school sites with using data to inform practices. I'm appreciative that we can have a frank and open conversation about how we can better support school sites." Her authenticity and candor paid off, and a few of the teachers from the site shared the value of using data and expressed frustration in that there was no consistency at their school or any process to help them use data effectively. One teacher added that she desired to better understand not only how her team was doing but would appreciate having ways of knowing how the school was progressing. This led to a visiting principal to share that it would be good to know if schools are having similar problems and how they may be overcoming these challenges because it would benefit other sites to have this information.

As the conversation unfolded it was becoming clear that data was needed at the classroom, school, and district-wide levels, and yet there were no agreed-upon processes or clearly defined practices to review student learning progress within or among school sites. Jacob had been waiting to see if a time would come to discuss the calibration tool with the group and, after seeing the conversations had opened this door, asked the group if the tool would be helpful. The teachers and principals took a few minutes to review the document, and a few began having sidebar conversations. Erin was interested in hearing these conversations and so asked if all could share their thoughts with the group. One of the teachers was in a fairly intense conversation with the site principal and, out of frustration, chimed up that she thought there was something missing on the calibration tool. She noted that there were no expectations for the district office's use of data in collaboration with school sites and that it felt as if all of the work was put on the shoulders of site principals and teachers. There was a long pause before anyone spoke, and then one of the visiting principals commented that principals received data reports at principal meetings. Another principal shared that it would be better if at

(Continued)

(Continued)

these meetings principals were to share information gleaned from the data and suggest district action steps and school site supports moving forward. Erin, as the only district leader in the room, agreed that this would be more productive and suggested that the calibration tool would be updated to include the role of the district team.

The principal who was to host the next school visit was in the room and made a suggestion to the group: "What if we do not visit my school next but instead schedule a time for each principal with a few teachers to meet at the district office and engage in this system-wide conversation of data-informed improvement?" Another principal suggested that meeting in leveled groups of elementary, middle, and high schools could be effective. Jacob agreed and added that meeting in smaller school cohorts would be better for managing conversations within groups. Erin liked the idea and offered to assign a district office liaison to each school cohort so that the issue of a perceived lack of district engagement with school sites was addressed. The teacher who had spoken earlier about the absence of the district role in supporting school sites commented on how odd it felt to be in the room with these decisions being made. She turned to the site principal and asked if she could attend this district meeting. Jacob inquired as to why she wanted to be at this meeting. The response of the teacher was simple yet impactful: "I have never felt that in my role as a teacher, I could have an influence on our school site processes and practices. But now I have an opportunity to do that and also help other schools and inform the district office. Why would I not want to participate in this meeting?" Erin smiled at the teacher, thanked her for her comment, and shared that more teachers like her were needed to help improve our schools and the district. She then adjourned the meeting and would follow up with all principals as to how this new meeting format would be structured and when it would occur.

In planning for this final meeting, Erin had asked Jacob to come to her office so that they could debrief about the school visits and flush out how best to design this new meeting structure. Jacob had been mulling this around and thought that a school leadership team format could be effective. Erin asked for more clarity as to what this would look like. At Jacob's school the leadership team came together each quarter and reviewed the data report to identify school-wide trends and patterns. Then the conversation focused on grade levels and content areas as well as individual student groups such as English learners and special education. After that, the leadership team came up with a few school-wide action steps that were shared during teacher collaboration time so that teacher teams could also create more specific action steps. This information was then shared with Jacob so that he had a sense as to how the school—and every team in it—was moving forward for the next quarter. Erin very much liked this process and suggested that a shorter version could occur at the district meeting with each school within every cluster sharing their insights and action steps followed by sharing to the whole group so that there was more clarity as to what each school was doing and what was expected to be achieved moving forward. Erin asked Jacob to share his process at the meeting, and she would have the half-day structured in a way that followed his format.

Two weeks later, the room at the district office was quite packed; every principal had brought two or three teachers to the meeting for reviewing data to guide school improvement. As suggested, schools were grouped into clusters with a district liaison assigned to each. Erin started the meeting by sharing the most recent data report and presenting district-wide trends and areas of growth. She then asked Jacob to provide an overview of the school leadership team process of data analysis and action planning. Schools were given an hour to review their data reports and create a few action steps for their school sites. Each school in the cluster was then provided 15 minutes to share their key insights and action steps after which another 15 minutes was allocated for questions and feedback from other sites. This process was repeated until all schools in each cluster had shared, and then 30 minutes was allotted to discuss common problems of practice and what could be considered promising practices.

The roles of the district liaisons were that of a notetaker and active participant of school clusters. They were also asked to share key insights and overall needs that were captured during the school

(Continued)

(Continued)

site sharing process. As this part of the meeting began, one of the district leaders asked to share an insight. Erin was intrigued and prompted the administrator to do so. After moving to the front of the room to take center stage, the district leader stated, "I've worked at this district for more than 15 years, and not until today did I fully understand the power of discussing data, sharing insights, and creating action steps in collaboration with school sites. I'm the one who creates the data reports and have always wondered how schools use them for their own planning. I appreciated today hearing some keen insights and action steps and also witnessed schools asking each other for ideas and assistance with overcoming real challenges." Afterward each district leader assigned to the remaining school clusters shared their appreciation for the day and communicated overall themes, action steps, common problems of practice, and a few promising practices.

Erin could not have been happier with the outcome of the meeting and also expressed her appreciation of teachers, principals, and the district leaders in the room. She then asked if this meeting structure would be a good replacement for the current principal meetings that were used to review data reports. A principal who had hosted one of the site visits spoke, "I actually liked having other school principals visit my site and was wondering if we could continue with these visits." Jacob, who attended all site visits, decided to share his thoughts, "I had the opportunity to visit multiple school sites, and I can't tell you how much I have learned that can be of benefit for my own school site." One of the teachers asked if this planning process could be done at individual school sites and then come to the meeting ready to share. She commented that it would be better to have more information that she could access only in her classroom. Erin then made the suggestion that every school site would complete the data analysis process and action plan at their own site and then come prepared to engage in a school cluster sharing process similar to what had occurred today. All agreed to this new format and seemed to look forward to a more structured process. Before the meeting ended, Erin passed out an updated calibration tool that now included the role of the district office (Figure 5.1). She asked all school principals to share this tool with their staff and share their comments and feedback at the next principal meeting.

Figure 5.1	Anywhere School District Data-Driven Inquiry Cycles
LEVEL	**COLLABORATIVE INQUIRY PROCESSES AND PRACTICES**
District Team	• Set a few goals and outcomes to create a strategic focus for improving student learning priorities. • Design high-impact systems of support for leadership, teaching, and student learning. • Develop collective expertise of principals and teacher leaders through high-quality professional learning. • Engage schools in identifying and overcoming problems of practice and sharing of promising practices to collectively improve teaching and learning supports.
School Principals	• Use data to focus school improvement efforts on student learning priorities. • Cultivate a culture that actively seeks out evidence of student learning to guide the improvement of school-wide practices. • Provide time, resources, and supports for teachers to build capacity using evidence to inform school site instructional practices. • Review school progress with teachers to determine how best to improve support systems for teaching and learning.
School Leadership Teams	• Analyze data to clarify the root causes of student equity and learning gaps. • Define student success indicators and evidence of learning to monitor progress of school-wide improvement efforts. • Guide the professional learning of teacher teams focused on the continuous improvement of teaching and learning. • Improve capacity of teacher teams to collaboratively plan instruction using timely evidence of student learning.

(Continued)

(Continued)

Figure 5.1 (Continued)	
LEVEL	**COLLABORATIVE INQUIRY PROCESSES AND PRACTICES**
Teacher Teams	• Analyze data to define the gaps in student academic skills and behaviors. • Create learning progressions and design learning tasks that are informed by evidence of student learning needs. • Engage students in short learning cycles with personalized instruction for mastery of essential skills and concepts. • Monitor evidence of student learning to collaboratively improve student tasks, classroom practices, and student supports.

© 2022 InnovateEd

Jacob walked to Erin and commented that it appeared that all of the previous site visits were building up to this final meeting. He felt that the challenges and barriers seen among schools would be resolved through this collaborative learning process. Erin agreed and could not help but wonder why it seemed like such a long journey to get to this point but then remembered that shaping culture, building capacity, and creating coherence is a process that must be done in collaboration with school sites. So she felt this was a good use of her and others' time. Seeing the other principals who had hosted site visits talking in the back of the room, Erin motioned them to come to her as she cleaned up the tables. She thanked them for their participation and was surprised to hear how each enjoyed the process, especially the resistant principal who did not want to change school processes or practices. The principal of the fragmented school was the most appreciative and commented that this new structure would be especially helpful for moving the school forward. Then the principal of the compliant school asked to host the next site visit, saying that doing so would allow the staff to become more proactive in leading this new work. Erin obliged and shared with the group that she felt that the district team had learned the most, and she looked forward to working more directly with school sites on finding new and better ways of improving teaching and learning district-wide.

Knowing the Impact on Student Learning Growth

A question commonly heard among educators, "What do we believe has had the most impact on student learning?" stems from the desire to gain insights as to what has worked best in advancing student learning growth. This is a reflective question that unfortunately occurs at the conclusion of an improvement cycle. It is an important conversation to have among teachers, principals, and district leaders; however, knowing the impact on student learning should begin with establishing agreed-upon outcomes for equitable growth in student learning. Hattie (2015) has referred to this as every student attaining at least a year of academic growth for each year of school. "Knowing thy impact" is not an afterthought; it is a forethought. All too often the dialog of impact is the last question to be asked rather than the first question of a collaborative inquiry cycle.

In *Districts on the Move* we had used an example outside of education to shed light on how organizations can define impact up front to guide improvement efforts. Southwest Airlines is the highest-performing airline in the United States and has experienced 47 years of profitable growth. But how? In 1972, when facing turbulent times and financial losses, Vice President of Ground Operations Bill Franklin was charged with solving the problems faced by Southwest Airlines. The solution was simply to unload and load passengers faster than the other airlines to get the planes back in the air; the now-famous "10-minute turnaround" (Hajek, 2015). The impact was that regardless of terminal location, airplane crew, or support staff, the collective outcome for knowing thy impact was whether the plane turned around in 10 minutes. What is the lesson learned? Focus on short-term indicators of success that predicate long-term annual growth in performance.

This reference returns to the concept of lag outcomes, lead metrics, and student success indicators. In this example of Southwest Airlines, the lag outcome is annual profitability reflective of the highest level of industry performance. The lead metric would be monitoring the 10-minute turnaround, whereas success indicators would be unique to the roles of each individual or team responsible for ensuring the timely arrival and departure of the airplane. All could measure the impact of their efforts using one simple metric and adjust their actions accordingly if in fact the short-term outcome was not achieved. The question for educators is whether there is an agreed-upon lag outcome for annual growth in student academic performance, clear lead metrics for monitoring progress and impact, and commonly understood

> Focus on short-term indicators of success that predicate long-term annual growth in performance.

indicators of student success that inform teaching and learning within and among classrooms.

Prior to the transition to the current accountability system in California that references a dashboard of annual performance measures (literacy, math, language proficiency, graduation rate, attendance, and discipline), Chris and his team at Long Beach had established a similar dashboard that focused district and school site improvement efforts. Although the performance measures varied, the intention was the same, ensuring that all school sites achieved equitable growth in student learning on an annual basis. Chris had ensured that these dashboards were commonly known among the school board, district leaders, site staff, and community stakeholders. In this manner, the goal for growth in student learning was known to all, and yet how to achieve this growth was determined by each school site through collaborative inquiry among site administrators and school staff. As had been referenced before, in Long Beach a collaborative inquiry process engaged every school site at either a 9- or 12-week period to review progress, measure impact, and guide ongoing improvement efforts. These timeframes provided an opportunity to gauge progress toward achieving annual growth targets and make adjustments and refinements to site-based improvement efforts. Clearly there were also shorter instructional cycles occurring between the periodic progress reviews with the intention being that short-term action steps would be informed by knowing the impact on student learning growth.

Another example of a district, one that InnovateEd had partnered with to assist in moving forward improvement efforts, was Moreno Valley Unified School District. Dr. Martinrex Kedziora, currently serving as superintendent, had previously been the assistant superintendent of educational services. At the beginning of the 2011 school year, the high school graduation rate stood at 69.9%, which became the top priority for district-wide improvement. In fact, the district goal was to ensure that every student graduated high school. Similar to Long Beach, Moreno Valley adopted an internal data dashboard with annual growth targets for each school site. The graduation rate along with a–g course completion and performance on Advanced Placement exams then became top priorities for secondary schools. At each high school, teams of site administrators, counselors, teachers, and support staff created action plans and reviewed progress every 9 weeks in a concerted effort to achieve the desired growth in student performance. Along the way lead metrics were monitored and student success indicators were reviewed to assess progress in student learning growth. At the conclusion of the 2018 school year, the graduation rate had been raised to 91.1%, a gain of 21.2%, which was also reflective of an equitable improvement for all student groups. In 2019 Moreno Valley was awarded the College Board Advanced Placement District of the Year, demonstrating equitable improvement in completion of rigorous courses among all students. And in 2021 all four comprehensive high schools were recognized as being among the best schools by *U.S. News & World Report*.

Another district that InnovateEd supported was Little Lake City School District in the Los Angeles area that comprises seven elementary and two middle schools. In a similar process, Little Lake had focused improvement efforts on ensuring all students were at grade level on the annual English language arts and math assessments. Each school had identified that more rigorous and complex learning tasks monitored by local measurements would serve as an effective improvement strategy for achieving this outcome. Each school created a site action plan that guided 9-week improvement cycles that ended with the analysis of local assessments and student work samples to calibrate student learning progress. The collaborative inquiry process brought together site administrators and teacher leaders alongside district leaders. The review of student work was intentional because this evidence reflected the work of students as they engaged in learning at the classroom desk. This also brought clarity to student success indicators: key cognitive skills essential for the completion of rigorous and complex learning tasks. The monitoring of progress every 9 weeks provided key insights of a few critical student success indicators such as close and analytical reading, precise use of academic language, and evidence-based arguments. These were critical insights for moving forward the work among teachers and school sites to continuously improve student learning at the classroom desk.

These examples serve as a reminder of the importance of establishing agreed-upon outcomes to achieve equitable growth in student learning and further reinforce the need to have recurring 9- to 12-week improvement cycles for monitoring progress and impact to refine action steps moving forward. In the end, the most important message is that "knowing thy" impact is not an afterthought but rather must be at the forefront of any improvement effort. Lag outcomes establish agreed-upon goals for improving student performance. Lead metrics serve as measurements for monitoring progress and impact at the end of recurring improvement cycles. Student success indicators guide the instructional practices and student supports that focus the work on ensuring all students demonstrate growth in learning.

Focusing Evidence of Learning on Problems of Practice

The concept of "problems of practice" has taken on a life of its own in the quest to clearly define improvement strategies for achieving growth in student learning. We have witnessed district- and site-level improvement processes identifying a singular problem of practice such as equity gaps among specific student groups receiving special education services. Not that it is a bad practice to identify students needing more support, but this strategy does limit the focus of improvement efforts because not all schools nor all classrooms will need to attend to this predefined and linear problem of practice. The unfortunate result is the perception among principals and teachers that there is only one problem to overcome, and certainly this will never be the case.

Cycles of evidence-based inquiry should instead focus on determining which leadership and teaching practices will have the greatest impact on learning among all students or, put another way, solving the problems of practice that are preventing equitable growth in student learning outcomes. We are referring to problems of practice among students, teachers, principals, and district staff because the improvement of practices always precedes growth in student learning. In *Districts on the Move* we referred to five key questions that can serve as a guide for engaging in such evidence-based inquiry cycles. These questions reframe the aforementioned scenario of a linear problem of practice to create a collective focus on improving leadership and teaching to achieve the desired impact on student learning. The common phrase "how will we know" is meant to serve as an evidence-based feedback loop to inform the collective efforts of teachers, principals, and district staff with building capacity and improving student learning.

1.   What problems of practice are observed among students as they engage in the process of learning specific content-based skills and concepts? Which cognitive skills for applying content knowledge are most important for students' learning, and how will we know?

2.   What problems of practice do teacher teams experience when engaging students in instruction designed to develop cognitive skills for applying specific content knowledge? Which instructional practices will better support learning, and how will we know?

3.   What problems of practice do school leadership teams encounter when facilitating job-embedded professional learning of teacher

teams? Which collaborative learning processes will better support developing the capacity of teacher teams, and how will we know?

4. What problems of practice do principals recognize as constraints for leading the improvement of school culture and practices? Which leadership actions will have the greatest impact on improving school-wide supports for teaching and learning, and how will we know?

5. What problems of practice do district staff encounter when supporting principals and teachers in their collaborative work? Which improvements of structures and processes for collaborative learning will have the most impact on developing leadership capacity, and how will we know?

If the intention is to achieve significant gains in student learning growth, then the process must begin with evidence-based inquiry at the classroom level and then move upward among teacher teams, school leadership teams, principals, and last to the central office so that the true problems of practice can be identified and commonly understood by all. Dr. Paul Gothold, San Diego County Superintendent of Schools, may have phrased the challenge at hand best in stating, "Our county office team has supported the improvement science work at the regional level and state-wide in California. What we have found is that a group comes together four times to define the problems of practice for the district without a systemic process for gaining key insights from classrooms within and among all school sites. A data-driven process, removed from daily instruction and the lives lived of traditionally underserved student populations, defines the problems of practice without having taken into account the specific needs of students and classroom teachers. The result is a linear problem of practice that focuses district improvement efforts when in reality there are more systemic equity issues to be overcome in the eyes of students, teachers, and principals."

If then we return to the five questions noted beforehand, then the challenge noted by Dr. Gothold is remediated through a more systemic approach for engaging in evidence-based inquiry. To do so requires that central office leaders in collaboration with school sites set the stage in using a more impactful process for identifying and overcoming problems of practice. Chris in his work in Long Beach has a great example of this in action. Because there was a district-wide and site-based approach in place for engaging in evidence-based inquiry, a request was brought to his attention from his nine-member cabinet.

The team desired to bring forth evidence that defined problems of practice within each of their divisions then present this information to their cabinet colleagues to ask for insights and assistance for overcoming challenges in an effort to improve district-wide systems of support. Each would have opportunities to present evidence that defined the problem, collectively discuss improvement strategies, and define how best to overcome the problems of practice moving forward. The key takeaway is that focusing evidence of learning on problems of practice is not an activity that occurs with one small group in a room to define the improvement strategies for the district and school sites. It must become the culture among school sites and at the central office in the form of an ongoing process of evaluating evidence of impact, clarifying problems of practice, discussing improvement strategies, and defining high-leverage action steps moving forward.

The previous example from Long Beach would be similar to school principals engaging in evidence-based inquiry to collectively define and overcome common problems of practice among all school sites. This could also be a process wherein teacher leaders at a school with site administrators focus their collective efforts on prioritizing and solving school-wide challenges. And certainly this would occur among teacher teams as the problems of practice with improving student learning in their classrooms was discussed to identify high-leverage instructional strategies and supports that would best accelerate student learning. When these problems of practice and improvement strategies are discussed within each school, shared laterally among school sites, and communicated vertically between schools and the central office, only then is there shared depth of understanding of the challenges at hand and viable solutions moving forward.

Continuously Improving Through Disciplined Inquiry

Continuous improvement always begins with analyzing evidence to define the problems of practice that are barriers to achieving equitable growth in student learning. The challenge for most educators is completing the subsequent phases of an improvement cycle because this requires a collective commitment among the members of a group or team. These subsequent phases include designing improvement strategies and identifying evidence for monitoring the impact on student learning, implementing the strategies, adjusting along the way to improve student learning, and finally, refining improvement strategies based on a common understanding of what worked best and why so that improvement efforts have greater impact on student learning moving forward. This evidence-based inquiry cycle is intended to occur at the classroom, school, and district levels in recurring 3-, 6- and 9-week cycles respectively with feedback loops that communicate progress and impact for informed decision-making. Such a systemic improvement process requires disciplined inquiry among teacher teams, school leadership teams, principals, and district leaders in the relentless pursuit of improving practices and achieving equitable growth in student learning. Maintaining these collective efforts over time can be a challenging task.

How then has Long Beach been able to maintain a systemic improvement process for the 18 years that Chris was superintendent and, most importantly, sustain these efforts after his retirement? This is uncommon because the norm is a loss of momentum over time and disruption of improvement efforts with changes in senior leadership. The answer, simple in concept yet complex in execution, is grounded in the work of Pink (2009), who has concluded that sustaining organizational improvement is driven by three factors: purpose, mastery, and autonomy. In Long Beach, systemic improvement efforts are driven by the common purpose of student equity. There is a shared belief and commitment for eliminating all barriers to student learning (access, opportunity, and support) to the extent that the closing of student learning and performance gaps is a moral imperative. A "loose-tight" improvement model exists wherein achieving equitable student outcomes is nonnegotiable, and at the same time, schools have autonomy to define the focus of improvement strategies toward achieving this outcome. School improvement efforts are supported by central office staff in an effort to further build capacity and help ensure success. This site-driven improvement process affords school staff the opportunity to develop deeper expertise and mastery of high-impact strategies of their own choosing. School improvement efforts are regularly celebrated by the central office in recognition of improved school capacity and gains in student learning so that the success of one school can be of benefit to other school sites (i.e., lateral and vertical collaboration and co-learning). In this way, systemic improvement becomes a district-supported and site-driven process that is sustained by the collective efforts of school staff as they pursue more impactful strategies for achieving equitable student outcomes. The common purpose, school autonomy with district support, and mastery of high-impact strategies combined with recognition and celebration fuel the ongoing improvement process.

This same model of sustainable improvement could easily be shifted to the school site level wherein the principal and staff agree on a common purpose, autonomy is given to teacher teams as to priorities for improving teaching and learning, and the mastery of innovative and high-impact strategies among teacher teams is celebrated and shared for the benefit of all staff. And to go a step further, this improvement process could exist at the teacher team level as individual teachers work toward a common goal, prioritize their own improvement efforts in support of student learning, and share the mastery and expertise gained by individuals with team members in an effort to support the learning of all students in every classroom. If this is the case, then why do we not see the disciplined inquiry and systemic improvement processes occurring within and among schools and districts at large? To answer this we must go back to the concepts of a climate of co-learning, a culture of collaborative inquiry, the capacity to co-lead improvement efforts, and coherence or shared depth and understanding of the work at hand.

Long Beach has agreed-upon structures, processes, and practices that guide continuous improvement through disciplined inquiry. There exists within and among school sites a climate and culture supportive of the work, the capacity to collectively lead the work, and a shared depth of understanding of the work and desired impact on student learning. In many other school districts and sites, this is not the case. To understand why we can look back 20 years ago, when Jay was a middle school principal and the fortunate circumstances of having Rick DuFour as a mentor. Over a 3-year period, the middle school was able to establish a 4-week evidence-based inquiry cycle that guided weekly teacher collaboration, monitored student progress within all content areas, and informed a tiered model of student support focused on equitable growth in student learning. Data on student academic growth, attendance, and discipline were used to improve teaching and learning practices and target student support systems. The school moved from lowest performing in the state to showing the most growth in the state among students of poverty and English learners. Most importantly, teachers were confident in their ability to co-lead improvement efforts and continuously improve and adapt practices to meet student learning needs. However, the successes proved to be unsustainable for several reasons. First, there was not a desire among other principals to learn from the work or consider ways of adapting within their own school sites. Instead, there was a culture of school autonomy and concern that the district may require school sites to establish similar structures, processes, and practices. Second, there was no direct involvement by the central office in the work of school sites, which prevented co-learning among school staff and district personnel to improve district-wide systems and supports. And last, when Jay left the school, the next principal shifted efforts to focus on new improvement strategies against the wishes of school staff who wanted to sustain the well-established school processes and practices.

Long Beach, in comparison, removed these limiting factors (the lack of principal co-learning, absence of a learning partnership among school sites and the central office, and dismantling of school improvement efforts by new site administrators as a result of not having agreed-upon district-wide structures, processes, and practices) by approaching the work as a systemic improvement process. Earlier in this book there was reference to the "mystique" of Long Beach, the essence of which comes from a common mindset and structured process focused on continuously improving through disciplined inquiry. In fact, this single factor is the missing link that defines the potential of schools and districts for achieving long-term success. The unfortunate truth is that no individual school can sustain the continuous improvement of teaching and learning through disciplined inquiry if there is not a systemic improvement process in place that engages all school sites and the central office in a mutually beneficial partnership of co-learning and co-leading.

The Path of Progress for Millikan High School

Alejandro Vega is the current principal of Millikan High School in LBUSD. His passion is serving students of color to realize their full potential. Prior to this, he served as principal at Cabrillo High School from 2009 to 2015 before arriving at Millikan, which has a lower population of underserved students and appeared to be supporting students well. However, after the first year at the school there were discovered to be hidden equity issues. Equity and achievement gaps existed, but these gaps were much less than most other school sites. Not all students felt equally connected to and represented by school activities and traditions. Student achievement was on target, but there was not a clear focus on the underlying equity issues and achievement gaps among certain student populations.

Beginning in 2016 and moving forward, the district-wide school climate survey indicated there was a gap between the connectedness of these unserved student groups. Uncovering the root causes of this

> No individual school can sustain the continuous improvement of teaching and learning through disciplined inquiry if there is not a systemic process in place that engages all school sites and the central office in a mutually beneficial partnership of co-learning and co-leading.

variance was seen as an important task for the school site. The pressing issues of poverty and trauma were much less at Millikan than other school sites, so there would need to be a way to attend to these equity issues without a strong sense of urgency. Seventy percent of students and families came from outside of the school community, which created a divergent mix of middle class and students in poverty. The needs of underserved students had not yet become a focus. School programs and academies seemed to have an identity based on these divergent student populations, which further heightened this sense of student inequity. Ensuring equal access to all instructional programs so that the student population was equally represented was part of the initial work.

The school staff were collegial and enjoyed working at the school site. However, there was an inherent hierarchy among staff as to courses taught and academies staff were affiliated with in the school. Moving toward a more balanced approach for the staffing of courses and academies was important to remedy some of the past practices that had an impact on existing student inequities. In reflection, these long-term practices occurred as a way to bring back the local community to the school site, and yet in retrospect, the impact was a tendency to tailor the school program to increase the enrollment of middle-class white families. Over time this practice had become the culture of the school site. The more than 30 buses of students that initially came to the school had shifted over time to a parental choice model in which students were driven by parents who wanted their students to attend the school because of its high academic achievement. Essentially, the school academic program had not adjusted to this change in student demographic. As the makeup of the school shifted to a higher-achieving student demographic, the needs of underserved student populations became less of a focus because this population had diminished.

Over the past several years there have been shifts within Millikan High School. This occurred as the instructional leadership team comprising teacher leaders, counselors, and site administrators began to take on these equity issues with more precision and focus. The staff is highly collaborative and competent with improving teaching and learning, so the emphasis was slowly and steadily pulling back the layers to better understand how to support all students based on their needs. Analyzing data and establishing goals to overcome equity gaps was most impactful because it allowed staff to clarify where the school could improve while providing autonomy for what to do and how to do it.

The purpose of the school has now begun closing achievement gaps by effectively supporting students with the greatest learning needs: an equity focus that drives continuous improvement. There no longer exist discrepancies in instructional strategies or supports among the six school academies. And staff have engaged in discussing implicit biases and participated in courageous conversations in an effort to better serve all students in the school. All students successfully completing a–g courses and being prepared to enter college has become the priority. Identifying, monitoring, and supporting all students at risk of not achieving this outcome is the focus of school improvement efforts. Millikan High School has evolved to have a laser-sharp focus on overcoming student equity and achievement gaps.

The Path of Progress for Signal Hill Elementary School

Tammy Lavelle was the principal of Signal Hill Elementary School in LBUSD from 2013 to 2018 and now serves as director of initiatives and accountability. Tammy has always been a data-focused leader, and her first step at the school was a deep dive into student achievement data to ascertain student learning needs. It was clear that African American students and students learning English as a second language had larger achievement gaps than English learners. So the initial priority was to engage the staff in further understanding these equity issues among student groups. However, Tammy quickly discovered that there was some resistance among staff to review current instructional practices within and among classrooms. This was counter to the fact that high-quality teaching and learning was occurring at the school site and appeared to stem from the past success of the school and the feeling among staff of already doing well.

Soon a priority emerged in the school that focused on formative assessment practices emphasizing clarity of learning outcomes and authentic engagement of students in learning tasks. This led to a focus on high-yield instructional practices with student feedback. Student learning began to accelerate, and learning gaps among students began to close. This led to an emphasis on small group instruction during guided reading as a common focus and agreed-upon practices within the school to be studied closely among teachers. By engaging in cycles of continuous improvement, staff over time began to collectively focus on the improvement of practices and student learning. And as a result, staff became comfortable with observing teaching and learning within each other's classrooms to develop precision of pedagogy. This would be akin to a lesson study approach structured as a continuous improvement cycle.

By the third year, a shift occurred in the design of school action plans from that of general problems of practice to overcoming specific learning barriers for individual students. These took the shape of 6-week inquiry cycles driven by a short-term action plan focused on improving practices and student learning results. These collaborative inquiry cycles became the "fly wheel" that drove school improvement efforts by monitoring student progress, recognizing improvement of staff practices, and celebrating student learning growth. When the achievement gaps among African American students and those learning English as a second language began to reduce, this further fueled and helped sustain the work among school staff.

The key lesson learned from Signal Hill is that a sense of urgency centered on achieving growth in learning for all students is critical. Schools need to identify a specific, high-impact instructional focus and engage in recurring collaborative inquiry cycles to improve practices and student learning results. As staff see the results of their collective efforts, the improvement process becomes embedded within the culture. By focusing direction, monitoring progress, recognizing the impact of teaching on learning, and celebrating growth in student learning, a culture of continuous improvement can be sustained by a highly committed staff.

Tips and Tools for Taking Action

In writing *Districts on the Move*, Jay had opportunities to collaborate with Dave Cash in his former role of superintendent and current role as governance chair of the USC Doctorate of Education program. Dave's comment about this previous work also rings true for developing schools to be on the move, "Capacity building is the holy grail for school districts to sustain a collaborative culture of inquiry that results in an organization focused on continuous improvement." The implication of Dave's comment is that it is not enough to support school improvement efforts. There must be a systemic improvement process led in collaboration with school staff, site principals, and district leaders for the purpose of building capacity and creating coherence in a way that achieves equitable growth in student learning and thus the reference to the "holy grail" for school districts.

In this chapter we have referenced three critical components for sustaining a collaborative culture of inquiry focused on continuous improvement: "knowing thy impact" on student learning growth, focusing evidence on problems of practice, and continuously improving through disciplined inquiry. These key factors are difficult to accomplish in of themselves; however, a systemic improvement strategy requires the effective implementation and integration of all three, which is a tall order for any school district or site. To accomplish this outcome, we have provided the following guidance for consideration to assist with creating a coherent system of continuous improvement.

Knowing the Impact on Student Learning Growth

Establishing goals for student learning growth, such as a 5% increase on the annual English language arts assessment, is a common practice among school sites and districts. What is uncommon would be predicting the impact of improvement strategies on the acquisition of student skills most essential for achieving a desired growth in learning. The former is setting a growth target for student learning, whereas the latter is knowing the desired impact of improvement strategies on student learning. The marked difference is that knowing thy impact requires teachers and leaders to make an explicit connection between the chosen improvement strategy and the desired outcome on student learning. This theory of action is at the core of the research by John Hattie in the distillation of effect sizes that denote the impact of instructional approaches on student learning. However, in this instance school staff engage in their own action research to discern the impact that school practices will have on achieving equitable growth in student learning. This is not an arbitrary selection of a growth target but rather an inquiry-driven process of identifying the highest-impact instructional approaches and establishing the gains in student learning that will be achieved by implementing these agreed-upon strategies. Michael Fullan in his coherence work has referred to this as "securing internal accountability" through the setting of specific goals with transparency of practice and results and a commitment to assessing impact so that evidence drives improvement efforts (Fullan & Quinn, 2016b).

So how do school sites actually accomplish this in action? A simple analogy may be helpful. Imagine that you have a pendulum scale that is a weight-measurement device with two hanging baskets where objects of equal weight are placed to get a net-zero difference. When the pendulum is balanced, then the objects on either side are of equal weight. Now let's say that a large rock sits on one side of the pendulum, and your task is to acquire the exact quantity of pebbles to offset the weight of the rock so that both baskets are perfectly balanced. Initially, you would make an educated guess and place the amount of pebbles thought to move the rock to an equal level of the pebbles. You would be wrong at first but would then continue adding pebbles until the desired equal weight distribution was obtained. What if you had a sense of urgency or only limited opportunities to balance the weight of the rock and pebbles? How would this change your approach? It would be assumed that much thought and deliberation would occur in understanding the size and weight of the rock and carefully selecting the right quantity of pebbles to achieve equal balance. This is the approach that schools take when working collaboratively to know the desired impact on student learning growth. Ana Gutierrez, principal of Lakeside Middle School, was noted in a previous case study as describing this process in her school as the following key action steps.

1. Engage in a gap analysis of student data and work products to clarify the distinctions among successful and unsuccessful students in the completion of rigorous and complex learning tasks. Identify the most essential skills for students to demonstrate for attaining equitable growth in learning. We would call this "studying the rock."

2. Come to consensus as to the desired impact on student learning in relation to the skills that are essential for growth in learning for all students. What do students need to be able to do and demonstrate to be successful, and what evidence of growth would satisfy this outcome? We would call this "knowing the impact."

3. Spend time as a staff studying the potential causes for this learning gap to discover the barriers preventing students from successfully using the critical skills in completing classroom learning tasks. Identify the instructional approaches with the highest possibility of overcoming the barriers to student learning growth. We would call this "gathering the pebbles."

4. Put the theory of action to the test by engaging students with the agreed-upon instructional approaches, and use evidence to understand the impact on student learning growth. Make adjustments and improvements to the strategies in an effort to collectively achieve the desired impact on student learning. We would call this "balancing the scale."

Focusing Evidence on Problems of Practice

As school sites define the desired impact on student learning, employ high-yield instructional approaches to realize this impact, and come to know the actual impact on student learning growth, what will be discovered are the problems of practices preventing further growth in student learning. The idea of focusing evidence on problems of practice is different than the typical approach of using data at a school site. Most often the analysis of data is used to separate successful and unsuccessful students, identify skill deficiencies among students, and place more emphasis on teaching underperforming students and reinforcing underdeveloped skills. This would be akin to a theory of action that reads "teach more and learn better." But what problems are we intentionally solving so that the efforts of school staff with improving teaching and learning have the desired impact? In returning to the reference to Lakeside Middle School, a focus on growth in student literacy led to the discovery of a significant problem of practice. It was found that there was much variation in how annotation markers (symbols representing how students mark up the text during close reading, such as underlining key facts and circling unknown words or phrases) were used among grade levels, content areas, and individual teachers. This was causing students to "relearn" how to annotate text among classes or when moving to the next grade level. Clearly students would never become highly capable of close reading and using evidence to defend, explain, or justify thinking unless this problem was solved. The discovery of the problem of practice was a direct result of focusing evidence on discerning the barriers preventing students from achieving the desired growth in literacy skills.

In the previous chapter we had referenced a series of protocols for creating instructional coherence and developing precision of pedagogy. The example from Lakeside is tightly connected to this collaborative inquiry process. But we can take a step farther by expanding the notion of problems of practice to include students, teachers, principals, and district leaders. This is essential because there is a tendency to focus only on the interactions among students and the classroom teacher to improve student learning when, in fact, the problems could be in the structures and processes used during collaboration time in the way that the school leadership team supports teachers in navigating the complexities of collaborative inquiry cycles; in the leadership of principals as they guide, support, and provide feedback to improve school practices; or even in how district leaders engage principals in clarifying learning priorities and monitoring school progress. We need to expand the concept of problems of practice to go beyond the walls of the classroom and consider how to improve the way in which leaders and teachers guide improvement efforts. To do so, we list in a shortened format a few key questions for consideration to focus evidence on identifying and overcoming problems of practices.

1. What problems of practice are observed among students as they engage in the process of learning specific content-based skills and concepts?

2. What problems of practice do teachers experience when engaging students in instruction designed to develop key cognitive skills for applying content knowledge?

3. What problems of practice do teacher leaders encounter when facilitating job-embedded professional learning of teacher teams?

4. What problems of practice do principals recognize as constraints for leading the improvement of school culture and practices?

5. What problems of practice do district staff encounter when supporting principals and teachers in their collaborative work?

Continuously Improving Through Disciplined Inquiry

Throughout this book we referenced the collaborative inquiry processes that Chris and his team at Long Beach had established with school sites to guide improvement efforts. If these ventures had been implemented over a few years, then we certainly would have commended the work. But in fact these agreed-upon processes and practices were maintained over the 18 years of Chris's superintendency and have been sustained after his retirement because other leaders support the continuous improvement of teaching and learning. We would call this "disciplined inquiry" wherein the culture of the organization has led to the adoption of an improvement process to become what is referred to as "the way we do things here." Sustaining continuous improvement requires a disciplined approach to inquiry that does not allow urgent demands, changes in policy, turnover in leadership, or a lack of momentum among staff to become a deterrence. District leaders, site principals, and school teachers work together to ensure the consistent and effective implementation of improvement cycles.

How does a school or district develop, maintain, and sustain such disciplined inquiry? When Jay began refining the work of InnovateEd to strengthen the approach of systems leadership coaching, he came across a resource that held the answer to this dilemma. The daily demands placed upon leaders and teachers is the culprit that can be thought of as the "whirlwind" that pulls all away from the critical work of improving practices to achieve growth in student learning. At first one would think that reducing these demands was the answer, but in reality they will never cease, and the best that any teacher or leader can do is dedicate 20% of work time to the leading of improvement efforts (McChesney et al., 2016). This could be seen as 36 days in a school year, 1 day a week, 1.5 hours per workday, or 12 minutes of every hour of instruction. However it is to be dissected, it is having a collective commitment among the members of the organization to engage in disciplined inquiry for this precious amount of time. And during this time, maintaining a clear focus on the desired impact on student learning to overcome the problems of practice preventing growth in student learning. The most critical consideration is whether this time has been calendared, held sacred, and continually reinforced in ways to deeply embed disciplined inquiry as a normal work routine among teachers and leaders.

Taking Action

In this chapter was the conclusion of the story of Anywhere School District and Somewhere School. In reality, though, it was only the beginning for district leaders, site principals, and school staff to lead the continuous improvement of practices and student learning results. The stage was set with the initial authoring of a model for collaborative inquiry cycles to inform the work at hand among the district, school, and classroom levels. As such, a systemic improvement process is designed to provide forward guidance, ongoing feedback, and evidence of impact for improving leadership, teaching, and student learning. When this model is designed, implemented, and refined through the collaborative work of district leaders, site principals, and school staff, the result is what Dave Cash referred to as "creating a collaborative culture of inquiry focused on continuous improvement." In Figure 5.2 you will find this tool, and in Figure 5.3 a blank template from which to engage in the process of co-creating a systemic improvement process.

Figure 5.2   System-Wide Inquiry Cycles That Guide and Support Improvement Efforts

LEADERSHIP LEVELS	ANALYZE EVIDENCE TO FOCUS DIRECTION ➡	DESIGN STRATEGIES FOR CAPACITY BUILDING ➡	IMPLEMENT ACTION STEPS TO BUILD CAPACITY ➡	REFINE PRACTICES TO IMPROVE IMPACT
District Leadership Team (DLT)	Set a few goals and outcomes to create a strategic focus for improving student learning priorities.	Design high-impact systems of support for leadership, teaching, and student learning.	Develop the collective expertise of principals and teachers leaders through high-quality professional learning.	Engage schools in overcoming problems of practice and sharing promising practices to improve teaching and learning supports.
Principals	Use multiple sources of data to focus school improvement efforts on student learning priorities.	Cultivate a culture that actively seeks out evidence of learning to guide the improvement of school practices.	Provide time, resources, and supports for teachers to build capacity with using evidence to guide school site practices.	Review school site progress with teachers to determine how best to improve support systems for teaching and learning.
School Leadership Teams (SLT)	Analyze data to clarify the root causes of student inequity issues, learning gaps, and underperformance.	Define student success indicators and evidence of learning to guide and monitor school site improvement.	Support the professional learning of teacher teams to continuously improve practices and student learning.	Improve capacity of teacher teams to collaboratively plan instruction using timely evidence of student learning.
Teacher Teams	Analyze data to define the gaps in student academic skills and behaviors for agreed-upon teaching and learning cycles.	Create learning progressions and design learning tasks that are informed by evidence of student learning needs.	Engage students in learning cycles with personalized instruction for mastery of essential skills and concepts.	Monitor evidence of student learning to collaboratively improve student tasks, classroom practices, and student supports.

(DLT cycles 9–12 weeks, principal/SLT cycles 6–9 weeks, and teacher team cycles 3–4 weeks)

© 2022 InnovateEd

Figure 5.3 Designing Systemic Collaborative Inquiry Cycles				
LEADERSHIP LEVELS	ANALYZE EVIDENCE TO FOCUS DIRECTION	DESIGN STRATEGIES FOR CAPACITY BUILDING	IMPLEMENT ACTION STEPS TO BUILD CAPACITY	REFINE PRACTICES TO IMPROVE IMPACT
District Leadership Team				
Principals				
School Leadership Teams				
Teacher Teams				

© 2022 InnovateEd

Taking Action 6

As this book was written a common theme of "being on the move" took shape and was reinforced through research-based improvement strategies, the story of Anywhere School District, and authentic school case studies. Schools that are on the move have an action orientation of forward movement driven by a moral imperative for achieving equitable student growth and a desire to create a coherent system of continuous improvement. The challenge is the divergence in starting points from which school sites need to navigate improvement efforts. For this reason, the final chapter has been designed to provide school sites with the guidance needed to create a coherent path of progress. And to this end, all roads lead back to the four key drivers of school improvement: clarity of focus, shared leadership, collective expertise, and continuous improvement (Figure 6.1). Central to these key drivers is collaborative inquiry, which is a common mindset and structured process for co-leading improvement efforts. In preceding chapters we laid out the purpose of each driver, framed how to attend to the most critical work, and provided tips and tools for high-impact action steps. Developing shared depth of understanding among school staff for each of the four key drivers is an essential step for initiating and, over time, sustaining school improvement efforts.

Figure 6.1 Four Key Drivers of Improvement

© 2022 InnovateEd

Lessons Learned From Chris Steinhauser as Superintendent of Long Beach

In Long Beach our secret was what Simon Sinek calls "The Golden Circle" in that we started everything with our "why," which was to prepare all children to be college and career ready. By building a culture of continuous improvement that encouraged innovation, experimentation, and flexibility, we were able to retain 93% of certificated and classified employees for their entire careers. We often referred to what we did in the district as "The Long Beach Way." This meant that every aspect of the school system, from the school board to the cafeteria workers, would do whatever it takes to ensure all students were successful. We never worried about policies at the state or federal level because these messages were translated to fit the culture of our system. In fact, we never deviated from our "north star," which clearly stated, "Every Student, Every Day." I would often tell school district stakeholders that as superintendent my litmus test was that we had a problem if I could not put my own children in the classrooms I was visiting. All parents want the best for their children, and I had a moral responsibility to ensure that all classrooms met my standard as a parent. I believe strongly that as leaders we need to model what we expect others to do, so I moved my own children from their upper-middle-class school to the school where I was the principal. When I was assigned to the school, it was the second lowest-performing elementary school in the district at the time. This modeling sent a powerful message to my staff, parents, and colleagues in that I was true to my word when I stated that all classrooms had to be good enough for my own children. I have used this mantra my entire time as an educational leader.

Although I have much to celebrate from the years serving as superintendent of the Long Beach, I know what I would do differently that would have accelerated student learning within and among all school sites. The hope is that these comments will assist other leaders with closing student achievement and opportunity gaps using the four key drivers of school improvement: clarity of focus, shared leadership, collective expertise, and continuous improvement.

Clarity of Focus: As superintendent, I learned early on that the goals I publicly discussed received a great deal of attention from all stakeholders and every school site. When I stated that all schools were to close achievement gaps by 50%, and that as a system we would reward schools that did so with fiscal resources and greater flexibility, it was amazing how many schools met the target. This is only one example that points to the fact that as superintendent I should have made more bold statements like these earlier in my tenure to better serve the students in Long Beach.

Shared Leadership: The central office is key to any school system in bringing about positive changes to student outcomes. I often publicly stated that the central office existed for one reason, and that was to support schools in their quest to enhance student learning outcomes. I did a good job of keeping true to this belief statement for the offices that supported the instructional side of the house but not as well with the classified departments. It wasn't until the last 5 years of my tenure that I reorganized how these departments supported school sites. By changing how classified departments provided support to schools, site administrators had more time to be instructional leaders because they did not have to spend as much time on noninstructional issues. An example of this new service was having all district budget analysts go to school sites on a regular basis to meet with site leaders and discuss the fiscal responsibilities site administrators. This new process proved extremely powerful for both the administrators and budget analysts. The analysts truly became learning partners with administrators and gave great suggestions of how to spend site resources in the most efficient manner. This process also allowed the culture of teamwork to blossom in support of the "why" of our school system.

Collective Expertise: The collaborative inquiry visits rely heavily on the use of data. In reflecting on how the central office supported schools in gathering their data, I strongly believe we should have done a better job providing site leadership teams with professional learning opportunities to become data analytic experts. This would be a wonderful opportunity to earn a district certificate that could be used when applying for support positions at school sites such as teachers on special assignment.

Continuous Improvement: During my last 5 years as superintendent, I started meeting directly with the leaders and middle managers of the Student Support Division who oversaw special education services. The purpose of these monthly meetings was reviewing fiscal efficiencies to reduce encroachment and identifying educational practices for improving educational outcomes for special education students. These meetings proved successful beyond my wildest dreams. We not only controlled the encroachment but served our most vulnerable students in a more inclusive manner. This is an example of an action that taken earlier could have saved the school system millions of dollars and accelerated the learning goals of our most needy students.

What must be considered in this work are the root causes of variance affecting school improvement: climate, culture, capacity, and coherence. Diving deeper into these four sources of school variance, we had created labels describing how staff attend to improvement efforts that included believers, doubters, idlers, and achievers (Figure 6.2). Doubters face competing priorities for student learning and believe that improvement efforts are essential for only some students. In addition, the limited expertise among staff and fragmentation or disjointedness of improvement strategies reduce the impact on student learning growth. Idlers also have competing priorities for student learning and believe that improvement efforts are essential for only some students, which reduces the impact on student learning growth. However, there is precision of practice among staff with a common schema and understanding of the work at hand. Believers have clarity of purpose and a belief that improvement efforts are critical for all students, but the limited expertise among staff and divergent schemas for the work at hand reduce the impact on student learning growth. Achievers have clarity of purpose and a belief that improvement efforts are critical for all students. In addition, there is precision of practice among staff with a joint determination for achieving equitable growth in student learning. Clearly the desire is for school sites to attend to the work in a way that develops the climate, culture, capacity, and coherence emulating that of achievers; however, the starting point will most likely be within the realms of believers, doubters, or idlers.

Figure 6.2	Impact of the Root Causes of Variability on Student Learning Growth	

	Believers	**Achievers**
High	Clarity of purpose	Clarity of purpose
	Critical for all students	Critical for all students
	Limited expertise	Precision of practice
	Divergent schemas	Joint determination
	Doubters	**Idlers**
	Competing priorities	Competing priorities
	Essential for some students	Essential for some students
	Limited expertise	Precision of practice
	Fragmented and disjointed	Common schemas
Low	**Capacity and Coherence**	**High**

(left axis label: **Climate and Culture**)

© 2022 InnovateEd

The purpose of the Anywhere School District story was meant to bring to life these root causes of variance affecting school improvement. In this regard, there were four school archetypes noted in this story. First was a compliant school whose staff are doubters who don't know how to lead improvement efforts. Second was a resistant school whose staff are idlers who don't see a need or reason to improve. Third was a fragmented school whose staff are believers who don't know what to improve. And last was a coherent school whose staff are achievers who know why, how, and what to improve. An overview of these four school archetypes has been captured in a chart that school sites can use as a tool to discern the current state of school climate, culture, capacity, and coherence (Figure 6.3).

Figure 6.3   Four Archetypes of Schools Within Any System

ARCHETYPE	CLIMATE	CULTURE	CAPACITY	COHERENCE
Compliant School **"Doubters"**	• There exists among staff a desire to be seen as supporting the vision of the school district. • The staff lacks a sense of urgency for changing practices to improve student learning.	• School staff want district guidance for planning school action steps moving forward. • Collaboration is seen by staff as a structure that organizes the work of teacher teams. • Staff do not have ownership of the work and passively engage in predefined tasks.	• The primary focus of the school is managing collaboration structures to achieve predefined student outcomes. • Staff do not have agreed-upon processes that guide the improvement of practices. • Staff has not yet developed capacity to co-lead school improvement efforts.	• The staff do not engage in the sharing of best practices to develop a common set of high-impact practices. • There does not exist a shared understanding among staff as to how best to engage in the continuous improvement of teaching and learning.
Resistant School **"Idlers"**	• There exists among staff a strong belief that the school knows what to do and how to do it and does not need support. • Staff overconfidence is due to the inability or unwillingness to question each other's thinking. • Staff appreciates school pride more than improving practices to meet student learning needs.	• There exists among staff a rigid mindset and lack of openness to deviate from a predefined school plan and action steps. • The talent and recognition of individuals is more important than staff collaboration. • Staff do not perceive a need for agreed-upon processes for improving practices.	• Shared leadership is not seen as essential because the school is recognized for doing well. • Staff is resistant to the changing of current school processes and practices.	• The staff desires to maintain autonomy by connecting the work of individuals to a static school mission and vision. • There does not exist a common commitment among staff for engaging in the continuous improvement of practices and student learning results.

ARCHETYPE	CLIMATE	CULTURE	CAPACITY	COHERENCE
Fragmented School "Believers"	• A lack of unity among staff stems from individuals wanting to maintain autonomy. • Protecting the status quo has allowed staff to remain independent in their work. • Staff do not yet value working together to get better together.	• Staff bring forth problems that prevent making decisions for moving the school forward. • Staff do not have common agreements as to how best to support student learning.	• There is a desire among staff to co-learn and co-lead, but there is not a structured process for deciding how to do so. • Staff have not developed the tools and skills for co-learning or co-leading the work.	• The staff are willing to create common processes and practices, but lack clear norms and action steps to do so. • There do not exist common agreements among staff for engaging in the continuous improvement of teaching and learning.
Coherent School "Achievers"	• There exists among staff a feeling of empowerment for making decisions that guide school improvement efforts. • A collaborative inquiry mindset among staff promotes informed and collective decision-making.	• There is a willingness among staff to work together, share ideas, and learn from others. • Staff have agreed-upon processes that guide collaboration and are comfortable facilitating teams.	• Staff have capacity to lead and improve the structures and processes that guide their work. • Staff have commonly agreed-upon tools and processes that guide school improvement. • The school has a collaborative inquiry process that is used by all for continuous improvement.	• A shared depth and understanding of the work among staff combined with collective commitments and agreed-upon processes ensure that the school continuously improves practices and student learning results.

© 2022 InnovateEd

Our goal is to provide practical guidance, actionable tools, and tips for taking action to support schools that desire to be on the move. To navigate a coherent path of progress, schools need an action plan to guide improvement efforts based on the four key drivers. We have suggested that there were entry points for this work based on the school archetype. Coherent schools with a staff of achievers will immediately take action, and so engaging in continuous improvement is the best entry point due to the comfort and familiarity with changing practices to improve student learning results. Fragmented schools with a staff of believers will take action at a slower pace, and so the entry point should be an emphasis on cultivating shared leadership. A resistant school with a staff of idlers can be supported to overcome uncertainty as to the impact of improvement efforts by leveraging the collective expertise among staff. A compliant school with a staff of doubters has the steepest hill to climb because inaction over time has created resistance to change and isolated practices, which can be overcome by creating clarity of focus.

Hesperia Unified School District has demonstrated a commitment to being a district on the move over the past 4 years of a partnership with InnovateEd. This district has been attentive to using the rubrics laid out in the book *Districts on the Move* and was equally receptive to using the rubrics in this book designed to guide all schools within a district to be on the move. In the words of Superintendent Dave Olney, "Engaging in and listening to the conversations of our district and school leaders around the four key drivers of school improvement provided greater clarity of district-wide progress. To witness our school leaders break into groups, discuss the elements of the rubrics, and then regroup to share a coherent message reinforced the work that the district has accomplished over the last 4 years, even through the pandemic, and clarified the work to be done. Even more impressive was the ownership—this is our work collectively."

What follows is the Schools on the Move Framework with rubrics and planning tools for taking action. It is important to note that this guide is a systemic improvement process that does not have a defined ending point and needs to be approached as a continuous improvement of leadership, teaching, and student learning. We suggest that the following tools be used by schools as part of a collaborative inquiry cycle wherein school staff assess current reality, define the desired state of improvement efforts, and design high-impact improvement strategies for moving forward. This inquiry cycle should, at a minimum, occur at the beginning, midpoint, and end of the school year. And in the interim, the work laid out in the chapters of this book for creating clarity of focus, cultivating shared leadership, developing collective expertise, and engaging in continuous improvement should be the focus of school improvement efforts.

Rubrics and Planning Tools

The Four Key Drivers of School Improvement

	CLARITY OF FOCUS	SHARED LEADERSHIP	COLLECTIVE EXPERTISE	CONTINUOUS IMPROVEMENT
Critical Success Factors	1. Multiple measures of student performance and well-being have been analyzed by school staff to create a strategic focus for achieving equitable growth in student learning.	3. School leaders and teachers have created agreed-upon structures, processes, and practices that promote co-learning among staff and guide the co-leading of school improvement efforts.	5. A coherent instructional framework adopted by school staff is used as a tool for developing collective expertise with integrating curricular resources, instructional strategies, and local assessments to accelerate student learning.	7. Annual measures of student academic performance and well-being are used as benchmarks to establish growth targets monitored by local assessments that inform school progress with improving student learning outcomes.
	2. A school implementation plan with clearly delineated improvement strategies connects student success indicators with high-yield instructional strategies and assessments for learning that guide school staff in the continuous improvement of teaching and learning.	4. School leaders and teachers collectively support school improvement efforts by serving as lead learners that shape culture, model co-learning, and use change knowledge to improve school practices based on student learning needs.	6. School staff engage in robust collaborative inquiry processes focused on engaging all students in rigorous and complex tasks using high-yield instructional practices informed by timely assessments of learning for the purpose of developing precision of pedagogy and improving student achievement.	8. Clearly defined cycles of collaborative inquiry, informed by evidence of student learning, create feedback loops at the classroom, teacher team, and school levels that guide the continuous improvement of practices and student learning.

	SCHOOL LEADERSHIP COMPETENCIES			
	• Creating a strategic focus for equitable student growth	• Nurturing a resilient climate of co-learning	• Creating instructional coherence	• Knowing the impact on student learning growth
	• Clearly delineating improvement strategies	• Cultivating a culture that embraces a collaborative inquiry mindset	• Fostering robust collaborative inquiry processes	• Focusing evidence of learning on problems of practice
	• Shaping improvement efforts through collaborative inquiry	• Navigating changes in practice to improve student learning	• Developing precision of pedagogy	• Continuously improving through disciplined inquiry

© 2022 InnovateEd

Creating Clarity of Focus

	CREATING CLARITY OF FOCUS RUBRIC			
CRITICAL SUCCESS FACTORS	INITIATING	DEVELOPING	ACCELERATING	SUSTAINING
1. Multiple measures of student performance and well-being have been analyzed by school staff to create a strategic focus for achieving equitable growth in student learning.	The school has multiple plans with disparate goals written to satisfy compliance with external expectations. Neither a clear nor strategic focus has been established to drive school-wide actions. Fragmentation and/or competing priorities are causing overload and reducing staff morale. It is not clear how the school site uses fiscal resources to target academic priorities and close student achievement and opportunity gaps.	The school uses annual measures of student performance to inform the selection of a strategic focus. A strategic focus exists in formal documents but is not widely shared and does not drive school site decisions. The school implementation plan was written to satisfy compliance with external expectations. The focus of school improvement efforts does not connect with school staff in a meaningful way due to competing priorities. Some budgetary decisions are aligned to the school improvement efforts to close student achievement and opportunity gaps.	Multiple measures of student academic performance and well-being are analyzed by school staff to create a focus for achieving equitable growth in student learning. A strategic focus exists in formal documents, is widely shared, and is beginning to drive school site decisions. The school plan, written to satisfy compliance with external expectations, is integrated with school improvement efforts. There is a strategy to reduce the number of competing priorities and eliminate distractors. Fiscal decisions are aligned to school improvement efforts to close student achievement and opportunity gaps.	Multiple measures of student academic performance and well-being are analyzed by school staff to create a focus for achieving equitable growth in student learning. A strategic focus exists in formal documents, is widely shared, and drives school site decision-making. The strategic focus is integrated into all school plans to coordinate and leverage improvement efforts. A process is in place to remove distractors, base decisions on evidence, and build coherence year to year. Multiyear expenditures are aligned to school improvement efforts and involve all stakeholders in ongoing decision-making.

CREATING CLARITY OF FOCUS RUBRIC

CRITICAL SUCCESS FACTORS	INITIATING	DEVELOPING	ACCELERATING	SUSTAINING
2. A school implementation plan with clearly delineated improvement strategies connects student success indicators with high-yield instructional strategies and assessments for learning that guides school staff in the continuous improvement of teaching and learning.	School leaders and teachers have co-created a school implementation plan to comply with perceived district expectations. Improvement strategies are neither clearly delineated nor coherently integrated in the school plan. It is not clear how focus areas are aligned with the school vision and goals to achieve equitable growth in student learning.	School leaders and teachers have co-created a school implementation plan to articulate their shared commitments for co-leading improvement efforts. Improvement strategies connecting instructional practices and assessments of learning to student success indicators are stated in school plans but are not coherently integrated to achieve the school focus and outcomes of improved student learning. Some focus areas are aligned to the school vision and goals for achieving equitable growth in student learning.	School leaders and teachers have co-created and collaboratively revised the school plan to ensure that improvement strategies align with student learning needs. Improvement strategies consisting of high-yield instructional practices and assessments of learning are coherently integrated to guide school-wide actions for achieving equitable growth in student learning. School improvement efforts are aligned with the school vision and goals and driven by the root causes of the student equity gaps.	School leaders and teachers have co-created and collaboratively revised the school plan based on an analysis of student learning at least every 6 to 9 weeks. The analysis of student learning priorities informs identification of high-yield instructional practices and refinement of assessments for learning, ensuring that improvement strategies are coherently integrated to guide school-wide actions for achieving equitable growth in student learning. School improvement efforts are aligned with the school vision and goals and inform the identification of problems of practice and promising practices.

© 2022 InnovateEd

ACTION PLAN FOR CREATING CLARITY OF FOCUS

CRITICAL SUCCESS FACTORS	CURRENT REALITY (based on the rubrics)	DESIRED STATE (what improvement looks like)	MOVING FORWARD (high-impact strategies)
1. Multiple measures of student performance and well-being have been analyzed by school staff to create a strategic focus for achieving equitable growth in student learning.			

180

ACTION PLAN FOR CREATING CLARITY OF FOCUS			
CRITICAL SUCCESS FACTORS	CURRENT REALITY (based on the rubrics)	DESIRED STATE (what improvement looks like)	MOVING FORWARD (high-impact strategies)
2. A school implementation plan with clearly delineated improvement strategies connects student success indicators with high-yield instructional strategies and assessments for learning that guide school staff in the continuous improvement of teaching and learning.			

© 2022 InnovateEd

Cultivating Shared Leadership

	CULTIVATING SHARED LEADERSHIP RUBRIC				
CRITICAL SUCCESS FACTORS	INITIATING	DEVELOPING	ACCELERATING	SUSTAINING	
3. School leaders and teachers have created agreed-upon structures, processes, and practices that promote co-learning among staff and guide the co-leading of school improvement efforts.	Formal structures, processes, and practices for collaboration and co-learning among staff are limited or may not exist.	School staff have an agreed calendar for collaboration and are beginning to formalize structures, processes, and practices for co-learning.	Formal structures, processes, and practices for collaboration have begun to promote co-learning among staff.	School staff have collectively created formal structures, processes, and practices for systemic collaboration and co-learning that guide 6- to 9-week inquiry cycles that inform the progress and impact of school improvement efforts.	

CULTIVATING SHARED LEADERSHIP RUBRIC				
CRITICAL SUCCESS FACTORS	INITIATING	DEVELOPING	ACCELERATING	SUSTAINING
4. School leaders and teachers collectively support school improvement efforts by serving as lead learners who shape culture, model co-learning, and use change knowledge to improve school practices based on student learning needs.	School leaders and teachers do not proactively or intentionally model co-learning themselves. School leaders and teachers do not apply change knowledge to guide improvement efforts. The collaborative work among school staff is fragmented, which promotes a culture of independent practice. Deep, trusting relationships are not present among school staff, nor does a culture of trust exist between school leaders and teachers.	School leaders and teachers participate in school site professional learning but rarely engage as learners themselves. School leaders and teachers rely on formal roles and structures to manage change. The collaborative work among school staff varies from shared responsibility to independent practice. Deep, trusting relationships are not consistent among staff members or teacher teams.	School leaders and teachers participate as lead learners and are beginning to make learning for everyone in the school a priority. School leaders and teachers are beginning to see their role as developing others and creating structures, processes, and practices that support co-learning among staff. School leaders and teachers are developing a culture of shared leadership focused on improving student learning. A culture of collaboration and trust is emerging among staff and beginning to promote the sharing of promising practices and overcoming of problems of practice.	School leaders and teachers model learning by participating as lead learners of robust capacity building within the school. School leaders and teachers have established a culture of shared leadership focused on improving student learning. A culture of collaboration, deep trust, and risk-taking has been fostered among staff to promote innovation and shifts in practice. Strong vertical and lateral collaboration and co-learning within the school fosters the sharing of successful practices and embracing challenges as opportunities for deepening learning.

© 2022 InnovateEd

ACTION PLAN FOR CULTIVATING SHARED LEADERSHIP			
CRITICAL SUCCESS FACTORS	**CURRENT REALITY** (based on the rubrics)	**DESIRED STATE** (what improvement looks like)	**MOVING FORWARD** (high-impact strategies)
3. School leaders and teachers have created agreed-upon structures, processes, and practices that promote co-learning among staff and guide the co-leading of school improvement efforts.			

ACTION PLAN FOR CULTIVATING SHARED LEADERSHIP			
CRITICAL SUCCESS FACTORS	CURRENT REALITY (based on the rubrics)	DESIRED STATE (what improvement looks like)	MOVING FORWARD (high-impact strategies)
4. School leaders and teachers collectively support school improvement efforts by serving as lead learners that shape culture, model co-learning, and use change knowledge to improve school practices based on student learning needs.			

© 2022 InnovateEd

DEVELOPING COLLECTIVE EXPERTISE RUBRIC

CRITICAL SUCCESS FACTORS	INITIATING	DEVELOPING	ACCELERATING	SUSTAINING
5. A coherent instructional framework adopted by school staff is used as a tool for developing collective expertise with integrating curricular resources, instructional strategies, and local assessments to accelerate student learning.	There is no instructional framework that connects curriculum, instructional strategies, and assessment practices across the school. Professional learning within the school is characterized by workshops and trainings that are disconnected from school site priorities. The school complies with district improvement efforts without attention to staff or student learning needs, which has created a culture of fragmentation and overload.	The district office provides the school with curricular resources, training on instructional strategies, and standards-based assessments that are meant to serve as an instructional framework for student learning, although connections between and among them remain unclear. Professional learning for school leaders and teachers comprises workshops and trainings on agreed-upon school site practices but does not inform the identification of agreed-upon, school-wide, high-impact practices. School staff members have autonomy as to how instructional resources are used for engaging students in learning progressions and classroom tasks.	School leaders and teachers have worked collaboratively to create a coherent instructional framework by integrating curricular resources, instructional strategies, and standards-based assessments. School leaders and teachers engage in job-embedded professional learning to develop collective expertise with high-yield pedagogical practices and assessments for learning. School leaders and teachers receive guidance and support from the district for the use of instructional resources to engage students in learning progressions and classroom tasks.	School leaders and teachers have collaboratively developed and periodically update a coherent instructional framework that integrates curricular resources, instructional strategies, and standards-based assessments. School staff collaboratively engage in job-embedded professional learning to develop collective expertise with engaging students in rigorous and complex tasks using high-yield pedagogical practices and assessments for learning. The focus of school improvement efforts provides defined autonomy for school staff to pursue innovative practices and develop collective capacity aimed at improving student learning.

DEVELOPING COLLECTIVE EXPERTISE RUBRIC				
CRITICAL SUCCESS FACTORS	INITIATING	DEVELOPING	ACCELERATING	SUSTAINING
6. School staff engage in robust collaborative inquiry processes focused on engaging all students in rigorous and complex tasks using high-yield instructional practices informed by timely assessments of learning for the purpose of developing precision of pedagogy and improving student achievement.	There is not a collective commitment among school staff to engage all four phases of the collaborative inquiry cycle (analyze, design, implement, and refine). Individual teachers and some teacher teams have informal collaborative inquiry processes for instructional planning and reviewing evidence of learning. The rigor and complexity of tasks and precision of instructional strategies are not being refined to support the active engagement and learning of all students.	The depth and frequency of collaborative inquiry cycles vary among teacher teams due to lack of consistency in completing all four phases of the inquiry cycle. Collaborative inquiry cycles are becoming more focused on pedagogical practices and student engagement of more rigorous and complex tasks. Evidence of learning is beginning to guide teacher teams in improving instructional practices and clearly defining student learning outcomes for each inquiry cycle.	Teacher teams are becoming more intentional about each phase of collaborative inquiry, having structured processes for instructional planning, reviewing evidence of student learning, and developing more precision of pedagogical practices. A school culture of collaborative inquiry is being developed as teacher teams engage in commonly agreed-upon inquiry processes. Some teacher teams engage in vertical articulation to inform teaching and learning.	Teacher teams within the school effectively lead collaborative inquiry cycles that guide ongoing, job-embedded professional learning. Structured processes for instructional planning and assessment for learning drive the continuous improvement of pedagogical practices and growth in student learning. School leaders and teachers collaboratively refine school site collaborative inquiry processes to support the continuous improvement of teaching and learning.

© 2022 InnovateEd

ACTION PLAN FOR DEVELOPING COLLECTIVE EXPERTISE			
CRITICAL SUCCESS FACTORS	CURRENT REALITY (based on the rubrics)	DESIRED STATE (what improvement looks like)	MOVING FORWARD (high-impact strategies)
5. A coherent instructional framework adopted by school staff is used as a tool for developing collective expertise with integrating curricular resources, instructional strategies, and local assessments to accelerate student learning.			

ACTION PLAN FOR DEVELOPING COLLECTIVE EXPERTISE			
CRITICAL SUCCESS FACTORS	CURRENT REALITY (based on the rubrics)	DESIRED STATE (what improvement looks like)	MOVING FORWARD (high-impact strategies)
6. School staff engage in robust collaborative inquiry processes focused on engaging all students in rigorous and complex tasks using high-yield instructional practices informed by timely assessments of learning for the purpose of developing precision of pedagogy and improving student achievement.			

© 2022 InnovateEd

ENGAGING IN CONTINUOUS IMPROVEMENT RUBRIC

CRITICAL SUCCESS FACTORS	INITIATING	DEVELOPING	ACCELERATING	SUSTAINING
7. Annual measures of student academic performance and well-being are used as benchmarks to establish growth targets monitored by local assessments that inform school progress with improving student learning outcomes.	External measures of student academic performance are reviewed annually to establish school goals for the year.	External measures of student academic performance and well-being are used as benchmarks to establish school growth targets for the year.	External measures of student academic performance and well-being are used as benchmarks to establish school growth targets that are monitored by local assessments throughout the school year.	External measures of student academic performance and well-being are used as benchmarks to establish growth targets measured by local assessments for frequent monitoring and communicating of school progress throughout the school year.

ENGAGING IN CONTINUOUS IMPROVEMENT RUBRIC				
CRITICAL SUCCESS FACTORS	INITIATING	DEVELOPING	ACCELERATING	SUSTAINING
8. Clearly defined cycles of collaborative inquiry, informed by evidence of student learning, create feedback loops at the classroom, teacher team, and school levels that guide the continuous improvement of practices and student learning.	The analysis of student learning evidence is dependent on scheduled school events and/or is dependent on the school assessment calendar. Cycles of inquiry may occur at the school but do not inform the continuous improvement of school-wide practices.	Scheduled events for analyzing evidence of student learning guide school staff in reviewing student performance on district and school site assessments. Cycles of collaborative inquiry occur at the school but do not function as a feedback loop to inform the progress and impact of school improvement efforts on student learning progress. There is limited sharing among school staff of student learning progress or the improvement of practices.	Cycles of collaborative inquiry among school staff are informed by lead metrics that guide the next cycle of inquiry with a common focus on accelerating student learning. There are structured opportunities for school staff to share student learning progress and improvement of practices. Feedback loops, generated by inquiry cycles, are beginning to demonstrate some evidence of improvement of staff practices and impact on student learning results.	Cycles of collaborative inquiry among school staff create feedback loops of the impact of improvement efforts on student learning results that guide the refinement of district services, school supports, and classroom practices for the next cycle of inquiry with a common focus on accelerating growth in learning for all students. Evidence demonstrates measurable improvement of staff practices and improved student learning outcomes.

© 2022 InnovateEd

ACTION PLAN FOR ENGAGING IN CONTINUOUS IMPROVEMENT			
CRITICAL SUCCESS FACTORS	CURRENT REALITY (based on the rubrics)	DESIRED STATE (what improvement looks like)	MOVING FORWARD (high-impact strategies)
7. Annual measures of student academic performance and well-being are used as benchmarks to establish growth targets monitored by local assessments that inform school progress with improving student learning outcomes.			

ACTION PLAN FOR ENGAGING IN CONTINUOUS IMPROVEMENT

CRITICAL SUCCESS FACTORS	CURRENT REALITY (based on the rubrics)	DESIRED STATE (what improvement looks like)	MOVING FORWARD (high-impact strategies)
8. Clearly defined cycles of collaborative inquiry, informed by evidence of student learning, create feedback loops at the classroom, teacher team, and school levels that guide the continuous improvement of practices and student learning.			

© 2022 InnovateEd

References

Aguayo, R. (1990). *Dr. Deming: The American who taught the Japanese about quality*. Fireside.

Bachmann, H., Skerritt, D., & McNally, E. (2021). *How capability building can power transformation*. https://www.mckinsey.com/business-functions/transformation/our-insights/how-capability-building-can-power-transformation

Bandura, A. (1997). *Self-efficacy: The exercise of control*. W.H. Freeman and Company.

Bayles, D., & Orland, T. (1993). *Art & fear: Observations on the perils (and rewards) of artmaking*.

City, E., Elmore, R., Fiarman, S., & Teitel, L. (2009). *Instructional rounds in education: A network approach to improving teaching and learning*. Harvard Education Press.

Donohoo, J., Hattie, J., & Eells, R. (2018). The power of collective efficacy. *Educational Leadership, 75*(6), 40–44.

Donohoo, J., & Velasco, M. (2016). *The transformative power of collaborative inquiry*. Corwin.

DuFour, R., & Eaker, R. (1998). *Professional learning communities at work: Best practices for enhancing student achievement*. Solution Tree.

Fritz, R. (2011). *The path of least resistance for managers*. Newfane Press.

Fullan, M. (2015). *California's golden opportunity: LCAP's theory of action*. Motion Leadership. https://michaelfullan.ca/californias-golden-opportunity-lcaps-theory-of-action/

Fullan, M. (2016). *Find your own Finland*. https://blog.google/outreach-initiatives/education/find-your-own-finland/

Fullan, M. (2018, May 9). Leading for coherence. [Conference presentation]. Second Annual Districts on the Move Summit, InnovateEd.

Fullan, M., & Kirtman, L. (2019). *Coherent school leadership: Forging clarity from complexity*. Association for Supervision and Curriculum Development.

Fullan, M., & Quinn, J. (2016a). *Coherence: The right drivers in action for schools, districts and systems*. Corwin.

Fullan, M., & Quinn, J. (2016b, June). Coherence making. *School Administrator*, 30–34.

Gallo, C. (2016, June). The power of storytelling. *Toast Master*, 16–19.

Hajek, D. (2015). *The man who saved southwest airlines with a "10-minute" idea*. https://www.npr.org/2015/06/28/418147961/the-man-who-saved-southwest-airlines-with-a-10-minute-idea

Hattie, J. (2015). *What works best in education: The politics of collaborative expertise*. Pearson.

Hattie, J. (2018). *Collective teacher efficacy (CTE) according to John Hattie*. https://visible-learning.org/2018/03/collective-teacher-efficacy-hattie/

Isaacson, W. (2011). *Steve jobs: The exclusive biography*. Simon & Schuster.

Johnson, M., Marietta, G., Higgins, M., Mapp, K., & Grossman, A. (2015). *Achieving coherence in district improvement: Managing the relationship between the central office and schools*. Harvard Education Press.

Lambert, L. (2003). *Leadership capacity for lasting school improvement*. Association for Supervision and Curriculum Development.

Marzano, R. (2001). *Classroom instruction that works*. Association for Supervision and Curriculum Development.

Marzano, R. (2006). *Classroom assessment and grading that works*. Association for Supervision and Curriculum Development.

Marzano, R. (2007). *The art and science of teaching.* Association for Supervision and Curriculum Development.

McChesney, C., Covey, S., & Huling, J. (2016). *The four disciplines of execution.* Free Press.

Mehrabian, A. (1971). *Silent messages.* Wadsworth Publishing Company.

Pearce, C., & Conger, J. (2003). *Shared leadership: Reframing the hows and whys of leadership.* Sage Publications, Inc.

Pfeffer, J., & Sutton, R. (2000). *The knowing-doing gap: How smart companies turn knowledge into action.* President and Fellows Harvard College.

Pink, D. (2009). *Drive: The surprising truth about what motivates us.* Riverhead Books.

Rogers, E. (1962). *Diffusion of innovations.* Free Press.

Sinek, S. (2011). *Start with why: How great leaders inspire everyone to take action.* Penguin Group.

Sivers, D. (2015). *Derek Siver's TED talk: How to start a movement.* https://www.youtube.com/watch?v=gxFt1BZiMTw

Sneader, K., & Singhal, S. (2020). *Beyond coronavirus: The path to the next normal.* https://www.mckinsey.com/industries/healthcare-systems-and-services/our-insights/beyond-coronavirus-the-path-to-the-next-normal

Westover, J. (2019). *Districts on the move: Leading a coherent system of continuous improvement.* Corwin.

Wiliam, D. (2018). *Creating the schools our children need: Why what we are doing now won't help much (and what we can do instead).* Learning Sciences International.

Index

InnovateEd
Building Capacity.

—on the move
JAY WESTOVER

and the InnovateEd team support district leaders, principals, and teachers to shape culture, build capacity, and create coherent systems that optimize student learning, achievement, and equity.

Is your system on the move?

InnovateEd is uniquely positioned to work with you to form a customized and impactful partnership beginning with your areas of greatest need.

Contact us for a **FREE** needs assessment: admin@innovateEd.com

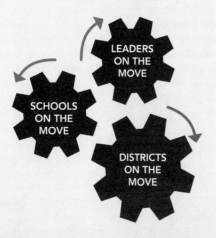

LEADERS ON THE MOVE

Cultivate a culture of continuous improvement and shared leadership.

SCHOOLS ON THE MOVE

Build the capacity of your site team to lead robust inquiry processes and utilize high impact strategies tailored to your site's needs.

DISTRICTS ON THE MOVE

Network with other district teams in facilitated, collaborative learning opportunities coupled with personalized coaching to implement evidence-based best practices.

Join the movement... **www.innovateEd.com**

A SAGE Publishing Company

Helping educators make the greatest impact

CORWIN HAS ONE MISSION: to enhance education through intentional professional learning.

We build long-term relationships with our authors, educators, clients, and associations who partner with us to develop and continuously improve the best evidence-based practices that establish and support lifelong learning.